The
Divine Folly

The Divine Folly

A Theology for Preaching the Gospel

Rubel Shelly

20th Century Christian
2809 Granny White Pike
Nashville, Tennessee 37204

ISBN: 0-89098-055-1

Table of Contents

Acknowledgments

As the Preface to this volume indicates, I was very reluctant to attempt it. My training is not in homiletics. I am not skilled as a preacher. I am a *teacher*.

With my reservations about the project ever before me, I sought the guidance of trusted people. In research and with preliminary drafts of the manuscript, they proved invaluable to me. Therefore my thanks to Tom Eddins, Mike Cope, Randy Harris, Phillip E. Morrison, Neil F. Christy, and Randy Mayeux.

Diana Gilfilen saw all stages of the manuscript through to preparation with her typical diligence. Bob Niebel monitored it carefully on behalf of 20th Century Christian.

Particular appreciation must be expressed to Jack Reese and Abilene Christian University. The university arranged for me to spend a week in research and writing on the campus. Interaction with students as well as faculty helped in the work.

Above all, I thank God for allowing me to share in the gift of grace called *preaching*.

Preface

During the middle decades of the twentieth century, relatively few books were written about preaching. The dominant text was still the Broadus text written last century. Preaching classes in graduate programs and seminaries declined steadily. Some people even spoke of the demise of homiletics as a distinct discipline. Many questioned the place of the study of preaching because it smacked of "how to" and seemed irrelevant to the larger theological tasks.

The last two decades, however, have witnessed an explosion in the area of homiletics. Major works are being published almost monthly. Graduate programs are discovering the centrality of preaching research and preparation.

I find, however, two areas that are frequently neglected. In the spirit of the times, most current works are highly specialized. The focus is narrow: particular methods, certain types of biblical literature, distinctive theological approaches. It is rare to find a book that examines the preaching event in breadth rather than singular depth.

Moreover, these works emphasize the preaching more than the preacher. Few address his motives and how they affect his method and message. Few examine his needs and how the Lord works through them to speak to people.

For these reasons, I find Rubel Shelly's book particularly refreshing. His work comes from a generalist perspective rather than a specialist. He addresses large issues. His brush takes broad strokes. His background is not one of academic expertise in homiletics (though he is greatly familiar with the literature). Rather he writes as a practicing minister facing enormous needs among the people to whom he preaches. His style does not come from carefully studied analysis of homilitics strategies. Rather he preaches as one committed to the clear exposition of the word, and he understands that any changes that may occur in listeners' hearts are due to God's workings, not his. His breadth of perspective is enormously helpful.

Moreover, this work is not really about preaching but preachers. It is easy, frankly, to construct sermons. It is much more difficult to construct preachers -- preachers who see their place under God's word and power. In an age that exalts the individual -- where talented and entertaining speakers can draw huge crowds -- the role of the humble preacher with godly motives and methods deserves greater emphasis. Rubel does us a great service in calling attention to the needs of the ones through whom God works to proclaim His message.

The context for this book is the annual Lectures on Preaching at Abilene Christian University in April of 1990. To be honest, we had to coax Rubel to be our first speaker. He truly did not think himself qualified. He suggested we find someone who had more specific homiletics training. But as you shall see, our choice of Rubel Shelly as our first lecturer on preaching was a good one. His inability to see his own value was one of the reasons we wanted him. His credibility comes through a godly life given completely for the sake of the Kingdom. It comes because he is a keen student of the Word and a tireless minister of the Gospel. With warmth and humor, with boldness and humility, he speaks of God's power to transform lives through the event of preaching. Whether or not you preach, you will find this book challenging and encouraging.

> Dr. Jack R. Reese
> Assistant Professor of Preaching
> Abilene Christian University
> Abilene, Texas
> February, 1990

THE DIVINE FOLLY

A Theology for Preaching the Gospel

Prologue

Presumptuous. That's the word which best describes how I sometimes feel in my role as a preacher of the gospel of Jesus Christ. Dare I, a sinner, stand before other sinners and hold out the prospect of eternal life? Still trying to find my own way through the maze of life, is it not shameless arrogance for me to offer to say anything to anyone else about life's meaning, purpose, and goal? When I think about what I do from week to week, I am overwhelmed by the audacity of it!

There is no way I could continue to do this work apart from the conviction that it is God's will for my life. A divine calling. A work from which I dare not withdraw. At an intensely personal level, I understand the meaning of Paul's words: "I am compelled to preach. Woe to me if I do not preach the gospel!" (1 Cor. 9:16b).

Yet I hasten to add that the temerity and presumption, the audacity and boldness of my work do not spring from personal conceit. I have not discovered the secret of eternal life. My searching has not unlocked the mysteries of life. To the contrary, it is merely that I believe in Jesus Christ as the Way, the Truth, and the Life. He offers eternal life as a free gift. He gives direction, meaning, and purpose to human existence. So, using the words of Paul again, I renounce the notion of any personal "eloquence" and disavow any claim to "superior wisdom." My boldness is in the Lord Jesus, and I proclaim "Jesus Christ and him crucified" as heaven's answer to our plight (cf. 1 Cor. 2:1-3).

People who bear the message of God have typically felt the sort of tension to which I have just confessed. Do you remember the confrontation between Amaziah and Amos? The priest of Bethel sought to rid himself of Amos' troublesome rebukes of Israel's idolatry and pride. In effect, he denied choosing to be a prophet and admitted to being at Bethel with some personal reluctance. "I was neither a prophet nor a prophet's son, but I was a shepherd, and I also took care of sycamore-fig trees," protested Amos. "But the Lord took me from tending the flock and said to me, 'Go, prophesy to my people Israel' " (Amos 7:14-15).

Have you ever watched with amusement as someone handed a timid deacon an announcement that a blue Ford with such-and-such license number was on the church parking lot with the lights on and the doors locked? He knew the announcement needed to be made, but he would have preferred not to get before the group to make it. He had enough decency to know that he should let the poor soul know his battery was going to be drained, but it obviously flustered him a bit to get before the microphone to communicate it. This is *not* the appropriate parallel to someone who feels constrained to preach the gospel of Christ.

Suppose that same timid fellow came upon a raging fire in a back room and knew that people gathering in the church's auditorium were likely to be hurt or killed by it if they were not warned immediately? There would be a much greater sense of urgency. There would be no whispering and looking around for someone else to make the announcement. Knowing that every second counted, he would step forward with boldness, make his announcement with clarity, and direct the people to move calmly but quickly to a safe exit. There is the better analogy.

"Professional clergy," a term I use to identify those people who go through the motions of Christian ministry without spiritual passion, may go about their work with the hesitancy of a deacon who must deliver a car-with-its-lights-on announcement. But a *preacher of the gospel* is someone who sees sure destruction ahead for people who do not know Christ. Thus he acts with a sense of urgency. He speaks clearly. And he points people to the one place where safety can be found.

In the opening verses of 1 Corinthians, Paul refers to the *gospel content* as "foolishness." He wrote: "For the message of the cross is foolishness to those who are perishing..." (1 Cor. 1:18a). "For since in the wisdom of God the world through its wisdom did not know him, God was pleased through the foolishness of what was preached to save those who believe" (1 Cor. 1:21).

The Jews, Paul explained, were demanding miraculous signs, and the Greeks were insisting on something which would fit the categories of Aristotelian logic. God, however, chose to offer salvation to Jews and Gentiles alike through a crucified Messiah. It made no sense to a sophisticated Greek, and it offended the Jewish notion of messianic splendor (cf. 1 Cor. 1:22-25).

There you have it. God chose to demonstrate his power to save through the powerlessness of being nailed to a cross. In humiliation and weakness, he conquered Satan, set the captives free, and opened the path to heaven. In what looked to all the world like a defeat, he conquered. In what human "scholarship" still reviles as foolishness, believers see the wisdom of God.

Knowing that pride is so antagonistic to all that is holy, God chose to save us through a person and a process which strips away pride. "He chose the lowly things of this world and the despised things -- and the things that are not -- to nullify the things that are, so that no man may boast before him" (1 Cor. 1:28-29).

We are not saved because we have either performed or witnessed with our own eyes dazzling displays of divine power. I've never seen a corpse brought back to life. Nor have I witnessed a miraculous multiplication of food at a homeless shelter. And I can't lead others to believe in Christ by duplicating the signs of the first century.

We are not saved because of our philosophic rigor or through invincible arguments cast in syllogistic form. For every argument, there is a counter-point. For every affirmation, there is a vehement denial. There are no knock-down proofs which will unfailingly convince every man or woman who examines them.

Salvation is in what Christ has already done at the cross. Not by what we have done. Or will promise to do or renounce. It rests wholly and exclusively on what a Jewish peasant did 2,000 years ago. And, yes, I know. To all the unbelieving world, that sounds like sheer foolishness.

The only thing I know that begins to compare to the foolishness of the gospel's content is the folly of God's plan for *gospel proclamation.*

If the message itself is likely to boggle the minds and harden the hearts of some, surely the method of its presentation will compensate. Angels will preach it. The saints of old will rise, walk the earth again, and tell the story of Jesus. Perhaps the Father's own voice will be heard from heaven occasionally. Wrong! The story of redemptive love has been entrusted to people like me. The treasure of the gospel has been placed in clay jars (2 Cor. 4:7).

Thus we are back to my beginning statement about presumption. What nerve it takes for people such as me to preach. Those of us who stand before groups -- whether small or large is utterly immaterial -- to preach Christ crucified are not essentially different from the people who hear us. They have equal or superior intelligence. Some are considerably more prayerful, more patient, more considerate. On any given Sunday, I preach to people whose character is better formed and whose faith has been more tested and purified than my own. So, I ask again, how dare I preach to them?

Preaching is no more a matter of merit than salvation. Both are entirely of grace.

Preaching is not something everyone can do, however. Just as the gift of athletic ability or musical talent is distributed to some and not others, so the requisite ability for preaching is possessed by some and not others.

Preaching is something that one should do only under a sense of divine calling. No, more than that, divine *compulsion.*

Then, daring to accept the work with fear and trembling, the preacher does his best to make himself inconspicuous while God confronts people through the Good News he announces. Thus Miller is surely correct in writing:

> No man has really preached until the two-sided encounter between him and his congregation has given way to a three-sided encounter, where God himself

becomes one of the living parties to it. Ideal preaching would go even one step further, where the presence of God becomes so real that the preacher himself drops almost entirely out of the consciousness of the worshipers, so that even as the preacher speaks, they and God seem to be left alone.[1]

In four lectures which follow, then, I speak to fellow-preachers about our mutual task. With no sense of being a model for imitation or a scholar with respect to the literature and methods of preaching, I seek to explore with you a biblical theology for our work. Along with you, I hope to discover insights which will make my own work more effective.

Then, in five sermons, I offer an attempt to apply the theology of preaching which has been discussed to an important section of biblical material.

---

[1]Donald G. Miller, *Fire in Thy Mouth* (New York: Abingdon, 1954), p. 18.

The Man

Introduction

The preparation to preach does not begin on Saturday night before the Sunday appointment. Nor early on the previous Monday in one's study. Nor even with the beginning date of your graduate education. The beginning point for preaching is with the formation of the man who will present the sermon. If we are not prepared as men to be God's vessels for the delivery of his message, scholarship, literary craftsmanship, and impeccable presentation will count for very little. The Spirit of God may use that lesson to achieve his purpose, but he will be able to do so only infrequently and with increasing difficulty.

> You have chosen a vocation -- or rather, Christ has chosen you for it -- which more than any other calling in the world depends upon the quality of life and the total witness of character which by the grace of God a man may bring to it. 'Preaching,' inquires Bishop Quayle, 'is the art of making a sermon and delivering it?' -- ahd he answers his own question: 'Why, no, that is not preaching. Preaching

is the art of making a preacher and delivering that. It is no trouble to preach, but a vast trouble to construct a preacher.'[1]

Preaching is inevitably a mix of message and messenger. There is no reason to deny it. There is no virtue in running from it. If some mistaken sense of modesty compels you to say that the power is entirely in the message and utterly without regard to the messenger, let the reality of your own experience force you to admit that you know better.

Moses was chosen by Yahweh to be his spokesman to Pharaoh. Anyone could have said what Moses said, but no one else had the background of education in Egypt, discipline in Midian, and calling at Horeb which made him uniquely the man to speak for God in that setting.

Paul was chosen by Christ to be the Apostle to the Gentiles. Any number of first-century Christians could have gone to preach at Thessalonica or in Athens, but none could have done it with the command of both Scripture and Greek poets or with the personal awareness of tension between law and grace which evangelization among the Gentiles would produce. God has not tapped people on the shoulder to do his bidding in the world without regard to their personal temperaments, backgrounds, and spiritual readiness for the work in question.

What was true in the lives of Moses and Paul is still true today. God employs people for his purposes in the world who are ready to be called by virtue of temperament, education, discipline, and spiritual suitability. And while

---

[1]James S. Stewart, *Heralds of God* (New York: Charles Scribner's Sons, 1946), p. 190.

God's powerful Spirit can use the sermons of men who "preach Christ out of selfish ambition, not sincerely" to lead honest seekers to salvation (cf. Phil. 1:15-18), such insincere persons are destined to be revealed for who they are and will become stumbling blocks to many. How many of us have seen churches set back for years by some scandal involving its preacher?

Does a "successful" preacher manipulate his elders for a raise by exploring a new work? He is serving himself, not Christ. Do stories of preachers becoming involved in affairs with women who come to them for counsel continue to surface? The problem is not with their homiletical skills but with their impure hearts. Has a preacher ever plagiarized a sermon or illustration? The same thing that took a candidate out of the race for the Democratic Party's presidential nomination in 1988 is a way of life for some who stand before people Sunday after Sunday to preach the gospel of Jesus Christ. If a nation has the right to demand personal integrity of its political leaders, the church has the right to demand as much of its spiritual leaders.

"Follow my example," urged Paul, "as I follow the example of Christ" (1 Cor. 11:1). Is this not the ideal pattern for every preacher of the gospel? He pleaded with his protege, Timothy, not only to preach but to "set an example for the believers in speech, in life, in love, in faith and in purity" (1 Tim. 4:11-12). It is interesting that Paul closed a section of personal instructions to Timothy with an appeal for him to guard both his conduct and teaching closely. "Watch your life and your doctrine closely," wrote the apostle. "Persevere in them, because if you do, you will save both yourself and your hearers" (1 Tim. 4:16). Many commentators have pointed to the order specified -- life first and then doctrine. Not only was the salvation of his hearers at stake but his own as well. Is it different with us?

Jesus warned his disciples against certain teachers whose orthodoxy was unquestioned but whose lives were grotesque caricatures of holiness. "So you must obey them and do everything they tell you," he said. "But do not do what they do, for they do not practice what they preach" (Matt. 23:3). Our generation has already seen too many preachers who do not practice what they preach. We need no more such heralds.

The key word of this lecture, then, is *integrity*. Anyone who dares to participate in the work of preaching the Word of God must guard the integrity of his heart and life. There is an old aphorism which holds: "Preaching is not a man speaking good, but a good man speaking."[2]

Personal Integrity

A preacher must exhibit the *personal integrity* of one who has been converted. He must know the Lord. There must be a sincerity and genuineness of Christian character about him for all to see. His credibility as a spokesman for the Lord must come from a Christ-centered and Spirit-filled lifestyle.

The work a preacher has been called to do is very different in nature from the poetry of Lord Byron or the painting of Picasso or the baseball playing of Pete Rose. His efforts are seldom better than his character.

---

[2]This maxim probably has its roots in the rhetorician Marcus Cato who defined the perfect orator as "a good man skilled in speaking." Cf. Edward P. J. Corbett, *Classical Rhetoric for the Modern Student* (New York: Oxford University Press, 1965), pp. 601-602.

In his 1907 Lyman Beecher Lectures on Preaching, Forsyth depicted preaching as an encounter, a real deed, a function of the great act of God which is the Gospel. On this view of preaching, souls are brought to stand before God in the hearing of his Word. To be revealed for who they are. To have grace mediated to the critical need of their lives. He added: "The act of Grace can never be conveyed by men on whom it does not act."[3]

Any person or situation to which you may point as an exception likely only confirms this rule. For the things we call "success" in those supposed exceptions are likely entrepreneurial flourishes of the sort which can gain both a church and a preacher a "reputation of being alive" when, in fact, God sees them both as "dead" (cf. Rev. 3:1). The passing of time generally reveals such a circumstance for what it really is. The "star" moves on and the church collapses, or both the man and the church lose their novelty and go into decline.

Personal spirituality must be the beginning emphasis for each of us who is a preacher of the gospel. The audacity of our standing to preach the Good News becomes perjury and hypocrisy if we are not taking the medicine we are prescribing for others. The idealism of the young must not become the cynicism of the veteran. If anything, we must become more consecrated to the Lord and increasingly sensitive to spiritual things with the passing of time.

I hope that you do not hear what I am attempting to say at this point in terms of legalism and perfectionism. My point is not that one must pretend spiritual maturity before entering the work of ministry. Neither is it that one must

---

[3]P. T. Forsyth, *Positive Preaching and the Modern Mind* (Reprint ed.; Grand Rapids: Baker Book House, 1980), p. 79.

conceal his weaknesses, deny his fallibility, or assume a posture which is smug and self-righteous. That is precisely the opposite of my point here.

While asking others to be open to the penetrating light of God's presence, you and I must also be open to it. We must not think that we preach to "them," for we first preach to ourselves. We accept the righteous judgment of God against sinners as a judgment against us first. With humility and penitence before God, we confess our own sin and seek daily grace for our struggles. Then and only then do we have the right to speak to anyone else. Then and only then do we dare to mount a pulpit.

The word here is *authenticity.* Preachers must be real and credible by virtue of our own genuine conversion. We must have turned both heart and life from the love and service of sin to the love and service of God. The people who know you best should be the ones who respect you most, for they know of your prayerfulness, your sense of burden for the lost, your compassion toward the broken and hurting people of the world, and your personal commitment to holiness.

The effective power for this sort of life is not summoned from within but is given from above. It is the power of the Holy Spirit who lives within us and bears fruit in the lives of those who yield to his presence.

When some people talk about the Holy Spirit and his presence in the life of a Christian, the first question they ask is: "How *high* did he make you *jump*?" That's the wrong question. The correct query is: "How *straight* is he making you *walk*?"

The purpose for the Spirit's presence in the heart and life of a believer is to produce Christ-like character. He is not among us to make us do bizarre and supernatural things, but to enable us to exhibit divine beauty in the characters we form, the relationships we live in, and the churches we build.[4]

Preachers sometimes lament that we "live in goldfish bowls" and that our lives are always being subjected to scrutiny. Indeed, Scripture warns of the stricter judgment which public teachers should expect (cf. Jas. 3:1). But what is there to resent here? When I have made that complaint, it was because there was something I didn't want others to know and from which I was hiding my own eyes. In a life of authenticity before God and men, there must be no concealing. No masks. No sham. No *self*-deception.

Preachers need to learn personal accountability in our spiritual lives. Within our own families, there must be openness and communication. Your companion for life must be your soul-mate, your confidant, your partner. The two of you must spend time alone, nurture your love for each other, and share the mind of Christ about your ministry. Your children must have a father, and they must know that they are more important to you than your books and papers. They need to learn how God loves his children by seeing the way you love them. Then, outside your family, you need a small group of people where accountability is real. These are people you meet with regularly, to whom you reveal your soul in candor, and with whom you pray fervently.

To stand and speak of spiritual things is not the heart of preaching. To live and breathe these things is its essence. Again, it is not that we need more good preachers so much as we need more godly men who can be called to preach.

---

[4]Rubel Shelly, *In Step with the Spirit* (Grand Rapids: Baker Book House, 1987), p. 41.

Thus we must be on our guard constantly lest we think that our sermons count for our spirituality.

> The man who constantly talks of certain experiences, and urges other men to enter into them, must come in time, by very force of describing those experiences, to think that he has undergone them. You beg men to repent, and you grow so familiar with the whole theory of repentance that it is hard for you to know that you yourself have not repented. You exhort to patience till you have no eyes or ears for your own impatience. It is the way in which the man who starts the trains at the railroad station must come in time to feel as if he himself had been to all the towns along the road whose names he has always been shouting in the passengers' ears, and to which he has for years sold them their tickets, when perhaps he has not left his own little way-station all the time.[5]

Unless you know your own sinfulness and live with the consciousness that you stand by grace, it will not be possible for you to minister that grace to others. Only one who has been broken and who has found wholeness at the foot of the cross can minister healing to broken people who live in a broken world.

Integrity With the Word

The person who preaches the gospel must exhibit *integrity with the Word of God.* He must be convinced that he has a means of access to the mind of God through Scripture, and he must be humble before, serious with, and growing in it.

---

[5]Phillips Brooks, *Lectures on Preaching* (Reprint ed., Grand Rapids: Baker Book House, 1969), pp. 25-26.

Our relationship as preachers to the Word of God does not begin with the identification and development of sermon texts. It begins at a deeper, more fundamental level. It is the foundation for the personal integrity and authenticity which were discussed earlier.

> The Bible is the supreme instrument in the cultivation of the minister's own soul. Behind every sermon there must be a man, and the primary function of the Bible for the minister is to produce that man. *The Bible is not for the minister chiefly a quarry of texts; it is rather the starting point from which he grows a soul.* And if he is not in the process of growing a soul, his ministry is spiritually doomed before he begins.[6]

A considerable amount of attention is being given these days to the issue of personal devotional life among the people of God. Historically in Christendom, though not in my own religious heritage, this has been a significant area of concern. The soul must be nourished. Roots must go deep. Hearts must not be denied the fresh and invigorating experience of God. Choose whatever metaphor you wish, but what some are being challenged to recapture and others of us are only now discovering is both real and indispensable. There are some personal spiritual disciplines which need to be cultivated in the life of any man or woman who would be spiritual. These include such obvious things as Bible reading and prayer. They may also expand to take in times of meditation and extended solitude before the Lord. And fasting should not be ruled out as an inappropriate legalism. Any one of these disciplines could become legalistic in

---

[6]Miller, *Fire in Thy Mouth*, p. 80. Italics added.

nature, but none needs to be. Each has its proper place in the cultivation of spiritual (i.e., Spirit-filled, Spirit-empowered) life.

> The purpose of the Disciplines is freedom. Our aim is the freedom, not the Discipline. The moment we make the Discipline our central focus we will turn it into law and lose the corresponding freedom.
>
> The Disciplines are of no value whatever. They have value only as a means of setting us before God so that He can give us the liberation we seek. The liberation is the end; the Disciplines are *merely* the means. They are not the answer; they only lead us to the Answer. We must clearly understand this limitation of the Disciplines if we are to avoid bondage. Not only must we understand but we need to underscore it to ourselves again and again, so severe is our temptation to center on the Disciplines. Let us forever center on Christ and view the Spiritual Disciplines as a way of drawing us closer to His heart.[7]

Willard writes of these disciplines and says:

> The disciplines are activities of mind and body purposefully undertaken, to bring our personality and total being into effective cooperation with the divine order. They enable us more and more to live in a power that is, strictly speaking, beyond us, deriving from the spiritual realm itself, as we "yield ourselves to God, as those that are alive from the dead, and our members as instruments of righteousness unto God," as Romans 6:13 puts it.[8]

---

[7]Richard J. Foster, *Celebration of Discipline* (New York: Harper & Row, 1978), pp. 95-96.

[8]Dallas Willard, *The Spirit of the Disciplines* (San Francisco: Harper & Row, 1988), p. 68.

My personal need for these experiences is clear to me. Just as a pianist can surely tell it after missing just one or two days of practice, there is a distinct difference in my ability to function as a spiritual person when these soul-nourishing things are neglected. Sermon preparation doesn't count. Time spent with the Bible in order to get ready for a class doesn't either. I have found that my day must begin with time before an open Bible. There I meet with God in preparation for what may lie ahead for me. There I read for personal insight, renewal, and direction for my life.

My day begins with a *One Year Bible* open to the readings for that day. I read with a highlighter in hand and mark verses, phrases, or single words which leap out at me. Then I pray over those highlighted sections. With my eyes scanning the pages and while asking God to scrutinize my heart, I celebrate my relationship with him and empty my heart to him. I use the ACTS "formula" for praying over what I have read. Beginning with the *adoration* of God for who he is and for what he has done, I *confess* my own need for him and my sins. Next I enter a time of *thanksgiving* for all his mighty works and for his goodness to me, to my family, to my ministry. Then I close with a period of *supplication* in which a host of needs in my own life and in the lives of people to whom I minister are laid before him.

Some people keep journals of their devotional thoughts. Others write out their prayers before the Lord. There is no single system which serves everyone well, but everyone would be well served by having a system of some sort.

Times for solitude and meditation are crucial, too. For me, these do not come with the daily regularity of a devotional time with the Bible and prayer. They take more

effort and planning, but they are always worth it. These
become critical in times of special stress. As surely as Jesus
had to pull away from the routine and rest from the press of
the demands being made on him, my pride is beginning to
allow me to admit the same need. Time for rest and renewal
is not wasted time -- and should not all be spent on the golf
course or at the lake. "Spiritual renewal" should not
become the code term for mini-vacations which the preacher
takes. Occasional events of secret and personal fasting can
help focus your heart on God and his will. In all these
episodes, the Bible remains central. It speaks to the one who
will later speak to others. It comforts. It rebukes. It
challenges to growth and maturity.

The occasional episodes of burnout most of us experience will be more frequent and more severe when we stray
away from the Word as personal sustenance. Thielicke puts
it this way:

> The preacher must read the Bible without asking in
> the back of his mind how he can capitalize homileti-
> cally on the texts he studies. He must first read it as
> nourishment for his own soul. For the light which we
> are to let shine before men is borrowed light, a mere
> reflection. He who will not go out into the sun in order
> to play the humble role of a mirror, reflecting the sun's
> light, has to try to produce his own light, and thus
> gives the lie to his message by his vanity and egocen-
> tric presumption. Besides becoming unworthy of
> being believed, he is condemned to consume his
> own substance and expend his capital to the point of
> bankruptcy. Because he is not a recipient, he must
> himself produce and seek to overcome the empty
> silence within him by means of noisy gongs and
> clanging cymbals. Thus he ends in the paralysis of

emptiness, and his empty, droning rhetoric merely
covers up the burned-out slag beneath.[9]

Then, of course, there is the integrity with the Word
of God which preachers must exhibit in the study, writing,
and delivery of the sermons we preach. We are heirs to
certain traditions. Some are healthy, and some are not.
Those of us who stand within the heritage of the American
Restoration Movement have a healthy tradition of respect
for and commitment to the Bible. A high view of Scripture
as the God-breathed word (2 Tim. 3:16-17) which came not
by the will of man but by the activity of the Holy Spirit (2 Pet.
1:20-21) puts us on solid rock. But the fear of some that
honest exegesis by a Christocentric literary-historical method
is dangerous puts them in quicksand.

Aristotle did not formulate an incorrigible logical
system, and the Bible was not written to accommodate
either his logic or any other Western thought pattern.
Locke's appreciation of Aristotle served him well, and his
English Empiricism was compatible with much of the system the great Greek thinker had organized. Since Empiricism stands opposed to Rationalism and since Rationalism
had been the cradle for the dominance of Calvinism, Locke's
challenging ideas were fertile soil for Alexander Campbell.
Using empiricist methodology and insisting that properly
reformed Christianity should "excite religion" through preaching the Word of God rather than simply cater to the prevail-
ing "religion of excitement," Campbell helped initiate a
wholesome and powerful desire for Scripture.

What Campbell started, though, he did not finish.
He did not give final expression to Christian theology. He

[9]Helmut Thielicke, *Encounter With Spurgeon*, trans. John W.
Doberstein (Reprint ed., Greenwood, SC: Attic Press, Inc., 1978), p. 10.

did not lay a foundation with the hermeneutic of command, example, and inference which would be definitive. In fact, the idea that he had done anything final with regard to Scripture and its proclamation would likely be abhorrent to him. The notion Campbell articulated insisted that men should be loyal to Christ alone as revealed in Scripture. Neither Campbell nor Locke nor any hermeneutical system devised by human ingenuity is inviolable.

Campbell's application of Aristotle as mediated through Locke may well have been providential for a time and for a purpose. But it was not conclusive, and the result cannot be venerated as being above challenge. It generated an inductive method of Bible study which assembled facts and marshalled propositions which could be used to discover the "Christian system." Thus the Campbellian emphasis on such items as distinguishing the Old and New Covenants, baptism, church organization, worship, and the like. For all its helpful results, however, that same approach also obscured the fact that the Bible is fundamentally narrative rather than systematic in nature. Contemporary scholarship has insights to offer which can serve as a corrective to that hermeneutic without losing anything of substance which it helped us discover. If a sounder hermeneutic reveals that we have been wrong about some matters, so much the better for us when we discover (and correct) those mistakes. If we discover that some of "our positions" derive from a human method of interpretation rather than from the biblical revelation itself, thank God for the liberation which comes of such a breakthrough.

Thus we are called to integrity before the Word of God in our study, exegesis, and exposition of it. There is no integrity in holding to a system of interpretation which is flawed. Neither is there integrity in allowing that only such approaches to interpretation may be allowed as will guarantee in advance that a select list of theological positions will be generated by them.

Dean Inge's famous counsel against marrying the spirit of one's own generation lest he be left a widow in the next is good advice to every preacher. Refuse to be wed to a system, a hermeneutic, or a creed for the sake of Christ. Exercise your Spirit-given freedom under Christ to pursue truth. After all, genuine faith is not believing whatever you wish regardless of the truth but following the truth wherever it may lead. That is the essence of integrity before the Word of God.

Integrity in Ministry

Having looked first at the man's conversion and then at his integrity as a disciple before the Word of God, only now are we ready to talk about a preacher's *integrity in ministry*. There is a particular task which a preacher has which no one else can fulfill. It is multi-faceted and, as will be pointed out in the second lecture in this series, finds different personalities committed to it and discovers one area of particular giftedness in some of those personalities and another area of special proficiency in others.

The common vocation which everyone shares who is really a preacher is bringing people to an encounter with Christ through the spoken word. Others counsel. Others go to the sickroom. Others weep with the bereaved. While these may be part of a preacher's experience, there is something he does which is distinctive to him. That something is why he is called a preacher. That same thing is uniquely his ministry before God.

The preacher's special task -- his *ministry* -- is what legitimates a claim so bold as Brunner's when he insists that wherever true preaching of the Word of God occurs, "in spite of all appearances to the contrary, the most important thing that ever happens upon this earth takes place."[10] That special thing which happens when faithful preaching occurs is an *encounter* between the Eternal Word and a human soul. Bonhoeffer pointed to the critical event involved in preaching with these words:

> The proclaimed Word is the Incarnate Christ himself. . . . [T]he preached Christ is the historical Christ and the present Christ. . . . He is the entrance to the historical Jesus. Therefore the proclaimed Word is not a medium of expression for something else, something which lies behind it, but it is the Christ himself walking through his congregation as the Word.[11]

Can we believe anything less about the preaching of the gospel and pursue it with the excitement of Peter or the commitment of Paul? And if we sincerely believe that preaching is an event of encounter between a lost soul and the living Christ, an event pregnant with salvific importance, can we ever be slovenly or nonchalant about a sermon again?

As a ministry, preaching will not bear trifling. The pulpit is therefore not a place for interesting but paltry matters. It is definitely no platform for personal beliefs, ego

---

[10]Emil Brunner, *Revelation and Reason* (Philadelphia: Westminster Press, 1946), p. 142.

[11]Dietrich Bonhoeffer, *Gesammelte Schriften*, ed. Eberhard Bethge, 5 vols., 4:240, quoted in Clyde E. Fant, *Preaching for Today* (New York: Harper & Row, 1975), p. 22.

gratification, or pop-psychology. The preacher diminishes his ministry by prostituting the sermon into a pep rally, comedy routine, or irrelevant lecture.

Preaching is a ministry of encounter, and sermons should have as their theme the Living Christ. The Bible, not newspapers or movies or today's best-selling biography of a business tycoon, is the source of preaching material about the Christ. Yet the Bible must be preached with an awareness of current events, theater, and personalities so that the meaning of Christ is made clear to today's circumstance. Depth in the Bible and breadth within the culture allow one to stand at the critical juncture of encounter in the pulpit. To use John Stott's wonderful phrase, a preacher stands *between two worlds*[12] and seeks to be God's instrument for relating Infinite to finite, Eternal to mortal. His role is "making present and appropriate to the hearers the revelation of God."[13] No challenge could be grander. None nobler. I repeat, *it is a gift of grace* to be called to this work. Yet none is more frightening, demanding, or intimidating.

One who undertakes this role must work harder at his task in life than the engineer, surgeon, or attorney. His work is more significant. It has greater consequences. It is a divinely commissioned ministry to be undertaken with passion. If the preaching of a sermon is more an event of encounter with Christ than the delivery of a speech, then

---

[12]"A true sermon bridges the gulf between the biblical and the modern worlds, and must be equally earthed in both." John R. W. Stott, *Between Two Worlds* (Grand Rapids: William B. Eerdmans, 1982), p. 10.

[13]Fred B. Craddock, *Preaching* (Nashville: Abingdon Press, 1985), p. 51. Elsewhere he adds: "Preaching brings the Scriptures forward as a living voice in the congregation. Biblical texts have a future as well as a past, and preaching seeks to fulfill that future by continuing the conversation of the text into the present." Ibid., p. 27.

those of us who preach must discipline ourselves to the preparation of those sermons.

Earlier I spoke of our need for personal devotional time with the Word of God. The warning then was that such times were not to be confused with time for sermon preparation. But there must be time for prayerful study when the specific goal is to prepare for preaching. With the other demands and pressures that go with local church ministry, it is difficult to find adequate time for sermon preparation. But we must remember our sense of calling and mission. If our *raison d'etre* as preachers is to enable encounters of the sort I have been describing to occur, then other things must wait. Prioritizing must occur. Preparation for those times of public delivery of the gospel must not be left to chance.

To separate my devotional time with the Word of God from my study and preparation time, the former happens for me in the den of my house. My devotional Bible and highlighter are in a drawer beside my chair, and time alone with God through Scripture and prayer begin my day. Shower, cereal, and coffee give way to the nourishment of my soul for the day which lies ahead. Then, at my desk in my study, the first hours of every morning -- my best hours for concentration, research, and preparation to preach -- are reserved for study and writing. I am rather slavish about it. It is difficult to reach me in the mornings. Calls other than emergencies will be returned after noon. Appointments will be kept in the afternoon. Visits will be made in the afternoons. Of course there are exceptions to the routine, but they are kept to a minimum with serious effort.

Students, factory workers, and professionals begin their day at a standard time and with a predictable schedule. Preachers sometimes waste inordinate amounts of time because they are left to set their own schedules and are accountable to no one. You can spend a lot of time unproductively sorting mail, reading newspapers, and counting paper clips. But we *are* accountable, both to God and to those who will be present to hear us speak on the Lord's Day. Integrity demands that we take our work as seriously as the student, factory worker, or professional person.

Is this realistic for preachers generally? Will churches allow it? This is only one man's schedule, and it will not fit the personality and peak times of others. But some sort of pattern for study and preparation is not only realistic but necessary for the preacher who functions faithfully. As to churches allowing it, that should be the least of your worries. When a congregation knows that its preacher takes study and preaching seriously, they will affirm him in it, cooperate with him in shielding those times, and register their appreciation of the outcome.

> If the minister extemporizes and takes what time he can find for his study then those times appear with less and less regularity. But if one gets his priority clear and sets about the business of building his study into a way of life then it is still possible, and doubly important. The importance is not only for the minister himself but also for the church which catches the seriousness with which the preacher comes to the time of preaching.[14]

If people in your congregation know that you reserve certain hours in your day for study, their respect for your work will increase. Knowing that you take preparation seriously, they will take the sermon itself more seriously. Thus preaching as encounter is all the more likely to become

---

[14]Gene A. Bartlett, *The Audacity of Preaching* (New York: Harper & Brothers, 1962), p. 137.

a reality in your ministry. By the consistent use of that time, you both discipline yourself to your task and educate the church about its significance.

Might you feel guilty at first? Yes. Will you have to make exceptions to your schedule? Of course. Could someone be offended that you are not available for a drop-in visit to kill some time he had on his hands? Quite possibly. But against the alternative of going stale and emptying the reservoir from which you function for the Lord, these are issues worth dealing with in their turn.

> After many years a man will still discover that one of the most exciting times in his ministry is the hour when he closes the door to his study to read, to medi-tate, to seek for understanding. It is an hour which has only one counterpart to it in excitement, namely, that in which he opens the door again to walk out refreshed and possessed of new insight to face the realities of human life with which he must grapple as a minister. That alternation, that going in and coming out, can be vastly rewarding, the pulsation of a living ministry.[15]

Integrity in Relationships

There is still an area of the personal preparation of the man for preaching which remains to be explored. It has to do with still another dimension of his integrity. There must be *integrity in the relationships* a preacher cultivates with those who will be touched by his ministry.

The people who hear us preach on a given Sunday are not our targets, prospects, or prey. And I will assume that we agree they are not to be our victims. They are,

---

[15]Bartlett, *The Audacity of Preaching*, p. 139.

instead, our brothers and sisters in human frailty. Just as Jesus had to "share in [our] humanity" in order to minister aid to us (Heb. 2:14), so must we share in the humanity of our congregations in order to minister aid to them. We are neither above nor beneath our hearers. We are one with the unsaved in the human condition. We are doubly one with those who are Christians, both one in human frailty and one in Christ.

The faithful preacher of the gospel of Christ must not only be deliberate in his study of Scripture but also in his sympathies with men and women. "The real preparation of the preacher's personality for its transmissive work comes by the opening of his life on both sides," insists Brooks, "towards the truth of God and towards the needs of man."[16] By this attitude of sympathetic involvement is not meant either a paternalistic or patronizing spirit. Brooks later explained:

> There is a great deal of liking for certain people in our congregations who are interesting in themselves and who are interested in what interests us. There is a great deal of the feeling that the clergy need the cooperation of the laity, and so must cultivate their intimacy. But of a real profound respect for the men and women whom we preach to, simply as men and women, of a deep value for the capacity that is in them, a sense that we are theirs and not they ours, I think that there is far too little.[17]

I have no right to preach the Word of God to someone from whom I isolate myself. If I am to succeed in

[16]Phillips Brooks, *Lectures on Preaching*, p. 26.
[17]Ibid., pp. 52-53.

helping someone under my influence to permit the gospel to inform her life, I must know something of its concreteness. If I ever gain credibility as a witness to the power of Jesus Christ to care for people, I must permit him to exhibit some of that care through me. And if I am to convince people that it is all right for them to reveal their vulnerability and sin to the body of Christ for healing within community, I must find it within myself to do the same thing with them.

Two experiences in my own ministry of the gospel stand out in this regard because they have been called back to me again and again by people who shared them. One was a Sunday morning during a particularly difficult period of my personal life. At the set time, I walked into the pulpit to speak. But I was so overwhelmed with the burden of my own pain that I could not. I simply could not fake it and mumble through a prepared talk. I told the people of my pain and confusion, confessed that I had nothing authentic to say that morning, and sat down. The other was the Sunday following my father's death from cancer, only three and one-half weeks after the diagnosis.

These are only two Sundays out of nearly 12 years of Sundays with the same church. And on one of them, the sermon was a non-sermon! In retrospect, I think I know why these two days have been brought up by so many people. They apparently let some people see my own vulnerability. My pride and "professionalism" may have kept some of those people at arm's length until those events let them through my defenses and into my heart, my pain. And it gave them confidence to let me into their hearts, their pains.

Unlike study time which can be purposed and pro-tected, times and situations like these cannot be created. They can only be reacted to out of one's identity before God.

No one will be denied his opportunities, though, for life is filled with challenge, heartache, and sin.

> The fact is that the church *can* become a kind of perpetual masquerade party. Everything is on the surface, and everyone is playing a role. Such relationships may go on for years without ever coming to the essential qualities of acceptance and forgiveness and the loving of persons as they are. Just as we put on our Sunday clothes to go to church, so many people put on a kind of Sunday personality especially tailored for that occasion. Small wonder that a minister grows restless and feels irrelevant in such a setting![18]

When someone dares to take off his or her mask with you, be genuine. Communicate the compassion and warmth of the Lord Jesus. Respect confidentiality. Confront with tenderness. Bear patiently. Direct to appropriate resources. Above all, love that person genuinely. Follow through. Keep on caring.

Craddock speaks of this as the necessity "that the minister really be a member of the congregation he serves."[19] Willimon refers to it as "the difficulty of being in two places at once -- the pulpit *and* the pew."[20] In whatever language you choose to express it, it affirms that the right to preach to others is derived not only from competence with the text of the Bible but from compassion for the hurts of people.

---

[18]Bartlett, *The Audacity of Preaching*, pp. 146-147.

[19]Fred B. Craddock, *As One Without Authority* (Nashville: Abingdon, 1979), p. 83.

[20]William H. Willimon, *Integrative Preaching* (Nashville: Abingdon, 1981), p. 22.

Gospel preachers are not Sunday performers. We are fellow-pilgrims with our brothers and sisters in the flesh who need us to care about them genuinely while challenging them to see that a personal encounter with Jesus Christ is the most critical need in every life -- including our own.

Conclusion

It is hard to improve on Brooks' definition of *preaching* as "the communication of truth by man to men" or "the bringing of truth through personality."[21] If this definition be accepted, even provisionally, then a study of preaching must begin with a study of the man.

If we then amplify this definition by understanding truth in a personal rather than a merely propositional way, the view of preaching as an encounter event between Christ and those who hear it staggers the imagination. It humbles the proudest spirit. It requires absolute integrity of those who are called to do it. Those who hear us preach are always asking themselves about our integrity, so we dare not fail to examine ourselves constantly on this critical point.

---

[21]Phillips Brooks, *Lectures on Preaching*, p. 5.

The Motive

Introduction
In the previous chapter, I offered a definition of preaching which holds that it is bringing people to an event of encounter with Christ through the spoken word. It is not moralizing or theorizing. It is not entertaining the troops or impressing others with ourselves. It is not merely the analysis of human need and public advice-giving. Other people do these things better than preachers can, and we should leave them their work so we can do ours.

Preaching does not work from the bottom up. That is, it is not the articulation of some human need, casting about for its possible satisfaction, and showing finally -- by a process of elimination -- that Christianity is a lead worth following.

Preaching works from the top down. It begins with a vision of God, shows the compassionate concern of God for his creatures, and reveals what God has done for us. From the explication of life from the top down, preaching brings men and women to a personal confrontation with the Living Christ and presents them the chance to confess and claim him unto eternal life.

This is not to say that a particular sermon will not begin with a reference to current events or by pointing to a need which people can acknowledge. Please don't miss the point here. We are not discussing sermon structure just now; we are examining the much larger phenomenon of preaching. A well-told story, an analysis of some vacuous human attempt at discovering meaning, the pointing out of some social evil -- all of these are perfectly in order for sermons. But the task of preaching is to do something much more significant.

Preaching establishes a mindset for seeing all of life from the perspective of eternity. It examines life through the eyes of God. It helps create the mind of Christ among the people who hear it.

Real preaching brings every issue and every person to the foot of the cross. It defines life in terms of the divine agenda of bringing all people to repentance rather than letting the world set the agenda. It exposes the emptiness of the world's way of thinking by the sheer force of contrast between the two agendas. If Harry Blamires is correct in saying that there is no longer a "Christian mind,"[1] the responsibility for losing our mind (!) surely belongs with those of us who are supposed to be preaching the gospel.

The Christian mind is not obsessed with hymn-singing and verse-quoting. It is a mindset which

---

[1]"To think secularly is to think within a frame of reference bounded by the limits of our life on earth: it is to keep one's calculations rooted in this-worldly criteria. To think christianly is to accept all things with the mind as related, directly or indirectly, to man's eternal destiny as the redeemed and chosen child of God." Harry Blamires, *The Christian Mind* (Ann Arbor, MI: Servant Books, 1978), p. 44.

> sets all earthly issues within the context of the eternal,
> the view which relates all human problems -- social,
> political, cultural -- to the doctrinal foundations of the
> Christian Faith, the view which sees all things here
> below in terms of God's supremacy and earth's tran-
> sitoriness, in terms of Heaven and Hell.[2]

Those of us who preach the gospel must think christianly, have the mind of Christ, see things through the eyes
of God. Otherwise, we can never lead others to a way of
seeing, thinking, and living which is spiritual. And at the
very beginning of the process of thinking christianly lies an
honest analysis of why we are about the task of preaching the
gospel. What are your motives for choosing to preach? Why
are you doing this rather than selling real estate or life insur-
ance?

I have facetiously explained that I wound up preaching because it was the only thing left for me in my family. My
father was an elder, my mother was a Sunday School teacher,
my oldest brother was a deacon, and the middle brother was
the song leader. For me it was either preach or be an atheist!
Just joking, you understand. But that would be a better
reason for preaching than some I have heard.

Several preachers have confessed to me that they
preach because they don't know anything else to do. They
have a college degree in Bible which has little "cash value"
on the job market. So they live in a church-owned house,
socialize with the church members, and deliver lifeless
sermons which have been plagiarized to church members.
They are bored and simply marking time. There is no fire.
There is no sense of purpose. There is no sense of divine
mission.

---

[2]Ibid., p. 4.

Some preachers are at their stations because they have found a cushy way to make decent money. One of these fellows in my acquaintance used to make jokes about his motivation for preaching. "I couldn't make this kind of money at a *real* job," he would say. Nobody in the world can be paid as well for doing so little as a hired churchman. So an avowedly lazy man kept getting fatter, continued laughing and glad-handing the brothers, and kept being asked to move every 18 months to three years by churches who were starving for the Word of God. He still stands in the pulpit and stumbles through other people's sermons. But he doesn't *preach*. His time in the pulpit is not an event of encounter with Jesus.

All of us have had our low moments when we realized that someone's compliment meant too much. At those introspective moments, we feared our egos. Some have set frivolous goals such as preaching for the largest church in town. Others have caught themselves playing church politics rather than preaching Christ. None of these motives is worthy of the calling to preach. No one who functions by them can be faithful to the task of preaching -- even if he is "successful" by the world's criteria of numbers, salary, and invitations to speak at special events.

Thinking christianly, what is *the motive* which justifies one being involved in the work of preaching? As a matter of fact, there is probably not a *single* motive sufficient to cause one to want to preach, to undertake the work, and to stay with it over the years. Since ministry is a multifaceted phenomenon, there are surely several reasons which underlie faithful preaching.

For the sake of distinguishing what I take to be the primary aspects of preaching, I would point to four things.

First, preaching is an intensely personal thing for me which is central to the living out of my faith in Jesus. Second, preaching involves a prophetic element. Here I am using the term "prophecy" in its fundamental sense of speaking God's will to a specific situation and not in terms of predicting future events. Third, there is also a priestly role which preaching fills in the lives of the believing community. Then, fourth, there is an element of pastoral concern for God's flock which must come through in preaching.

Just as these elements of the preaching ministry overlap and intertwine, so do the motives underlying them. For the sake of this discussion, however, I want to isolate and discuss a particular motive which seems most naturally linked with each of these aspects of our work.

A Personal Motive

How can we not admit that part of the motive underlying the decision to preach is intensely *personal*?

A psychoanalyst might help us find some of the deeper personal motives that cause some to first entertain the possibility of preaching. It might be something so obvious in the early lives of many of us as being influenced by a preacher. Looking up to preachers. Wanting to have the respect from others that we were taught to give to preachers. Or it might be something so complex as a guilt-ridden attempt to atone for a moral failure. Let it even be granted that some choose to preach in order to satisfy some neurosis or "messiah complex."

What I have in mind as a personal motivation for preaching, however, is different from these. It is a pure and spiritual motive which is nonetheless intensely personal. It even has the capacity to emerge in the life of one who began to preach for some unworthy personal motive, overshadow and crowd out that motive, and sanctify a ministry to God's glory.

This most personal motive for preaching is gratitude for grace received. Such a motive is the ground of humility. It is the basis for accepting others and being patient with them. It is the fundamental insight necessary for preaching Good News as opposed to dispensing good advice.

No one will preach the gospel well who has not been broken before the Lord. The pulpit is no place for arrogant preening. It is not a soap box. It is not a judge's bench without a gavel. And it is not a defensive platform from behind which an insecure man will build himself up by tearing others down. Oh, the pulpit can be used for these purposes. But God did not create it for such things.

Have you ever paid much attention to the architecture of pulpits? Some are elevated above everything else in the room. Some really do look like sections of a judge's bench. And some are massive and imposing. Do we need such perches for our work? Do we want to tower over our audiences, to intimidate them? Do we want such imposing barriers between us and the people to whom we speak?

Of course one can cultivate a personality and style which belie architectural statements. Some of us have chosen actually to rearrange the furniture. To put a communion table at a more central and elevated place than the pulpit. To replace massive pulpits with "friendlier" ones. Or to speak directly to people without the intervening presence of a pulpit. However you choose to communicate it architecturally, preaching demands an alternative to authoritarianism. That alternative style is generated by an awareness of grace as the foundation of the preacher's life and work.

Niles once said of himself:

> That is what I am. I am a sinner for whom Jesus died. I am just one of those who has been loved of God in Jesus at the cross. That is the central truth about me. All the rest is peripheral.[3]

Can any preacher of the gospel say less of himself and see himself in true perspective? I am neither above nor beneath those to whom I preach. We are in the same condition before a Holy God. Hopeless without grace. Helpless without Christ. Homeless without heaven. "We are *worthy* of being believed only as we are aware of our unworthiness," said Barth.

> There is no such thing as *convincing* utterance about God except as Christian preaching feels its *need*, takes up its *cross*, and asks the *question* which God demands in order to be able to answer it. From this need we may not hope to flee.[4]

One who has been broken before the cross, lifted by grace into heavenly realms, and allowed by God to participate in the ongoing work of redemption by preaching Christ has motivation to stay at his work. Confessing his own sinfulness, his humility will not let him take credit for God's successes or live a pompous piety. At the same time, since he sees his role as the faithful presentation of the gospel rather than building a "great church" (i.e., numbers) where

---

[3]D. T. Niles, *Preaching the Gospel of the Resurrection* (Philadelphia: Westminster Press, 1953), p. 45.

[4]Karl Barth, *The Word of God and the Word of Man*, trans. Douglas Horton (Grand Rapids: Zondervan Publishing House, 1935), p. 129.

he must be the "star," he is neither envious nor despairing in relation to others.

Because he understands that he stands by grace and because he is motivated for his ministry by gratitude for that grace, this sort of preacher is able to accept others for who they are. He can avoid catering to the few who are wealthy or powerful. He can be involved in the lives of the poor and weak. He can be patient with the brother or sister whose spiritual life is coming along slowly or with painful inconsistency.

Because he understands that his own personal relationship with God is by grace, he has the fundamental insight which is necessary to preach the gospel faithfully. He no longer blusters moral strictures and pessimistic judgments in hope of hearing someone promise, "I will do better, preacher," but lifts up Christ, allows sin to stand self-condemned in the brilliant light of his perfect holiness, and proclaims the optimistic promise that sin can be forgiven in hope of hearing someone exclaim, "Yes, I see him dying there for me!" That is the message of grace. And it is truly amazing.

Think of Paul's personal motivation to his apostolic ministry by grace. "But by the grace of God I am what I am, and his grace to me was not without effect," he said. "No, I worked harder than all of them -- yet not I, but the grace of God that was with me" (1 Cor. 15:10). Having admitted in the previous verse that he did not "deserve" to be an apostle because of his persecutions against the church of God, he now confesses that all for him is of grace. Not his salvation only, but his special ministry. May we not confess the same? For Paul, it seems clear from this verse that

> ... his concern is to say something about his own ministry as such, including his having come to Corinth with the gospel. To make sure that he is not misunderstood, he quickly qualifies with 'yet not I, but the grace of God that was with me.' That is, even my intense labors in the gospel are ultimately not the result of a personal need to compensate God for his grace, but are themselves the reflection of that grace at work in my life. Thus, in Pauline theology, even though his labor is a response to grace, it is more properly seen as the effect of grace. All is of grace; nothing is deserved. Neither therefore can he lay claim to his own ministry nor can they reject it; it is God's activity in him in their behalf.[5]

Is it wrong for us to feel the same way about our special ministry of preaching? That it is rooted in grace? That it is sustained by grace? That it is a means of mediating grace? And if we can believe these things about our work of preaching the gospel, we can also believe that it is God's activity in us on the behalf of men. Thus neither pride nor despair defeats it.

My salvation and my ministry of preaching are both gifts of grace, and gratitude for that grace keeps me at tasks nothing else could.

A Prophetic Motive

There is a second element of the total motive which underlies preaching which relates to the *prophetic* element of our ministry. The prophet, whether in the Old Testament or the New Testament, was always less a man with insight

---

[5]Gordon D. Fee, *The First Epistle to the Corinthians* (Grand Rapids: William B. Eerdmans Publishing Company, 1987), pp. 735-736.

into the future than a man with critical insight into his own time and life situation. He could speak a word from God which was appropriate to the time. While we fill our prophetic role through the study and application of their Spirit-guided words to our own time, it is unequivocally a part of faithful gospel preaching to stand and speak a word of challenge, rebuke, or commitment.

As with the Old Testament prophets, those of us who preach are not merely conveying words of heavenly origin but making God known. "In speaking, the prophet reveals God. . . . The authority of the prophet is in the Presence his words reveal."[6] The prophetic motivation for preaching is a clear and distinct sense of call from God. Yes, I believe that God *calls* men to preach the gospel. No, I don't believe his call to men today is so direct and unmistakable as those which came to Jeremiah or Paul. But unless one can serve God in preaching with a positive sense of commission from him for the task, he will not remain faithful in the trying times which are sure to come.

How does God call someone to preach? What sorts of things should cause someone to consider giving himself to the ministry of the gospel?

I have wondered why there is not a single, definitive biblical text on this point. At first blush, it would appear that such a text would make life much simpler for all of us who have ever considered preaching. But maybe that is precisely why there is no such text. Who said life ought to be without struggle or ambiguity for us? The people we preach to do not have the luxury of accepting their life roles without stress. Neither should we. At best, I can only give you my

---

[6]Abraham J. Heschel, *The Prophets*, vol. 1 (New York: Harper & Row, 1962), p. 22.

opinion about the elements of a divine call to preach. In doing so, I will be sharing some of the struggle and its results from my own life.

First, there is obviously the matter of one's personal temperament and gifts from God. Why do you suppose Magic Johnson chose to play basketball -- and I didn't? You get the point, don't you? Some things which are givens in a person tend him toward certain possibilities and away from others. If the spiritual gifts of 1 Corinthians 12 are chiefly those which came to certain people by supernatural endowment, I believe those listed in Romans 12:6-8 are found generally among the people of God. The specific gifts of prophesying, teaching, and perhaps leadership would appear on the very surface of things to be relevant to preaching. One has a non-miraculous gift of prophecy who is sensitive to people and circumstances and has insight into the Word of God to bring biblical teaching to bear on them in a practical way. Teaching is the ability to lead others through Scripture in compelling, faithful, and helpful ways. Leadership is the gift of being able to bring others together around worthwhile ideas and works and then enabling them to carry through with them.

Second, there must be a degree of personal desire and motivation to the work of preaching. Larry Bird does not have the natural gifts of Magic Johnson, but he had a desire to play basketball which has caused him to work harder at doing things which came more easily for another. The same thing may happen with regard to someone's motivation to serve God through preaching. I have known men who had lesser natural gifts or talent for public speaking or academic prowess who nevertheless had such hearts for God and men that they had to put far more effort into certain parts of their ministry than others for whom it came more easily. Even for the one who has obvious giftedness, however, likely some degree of desire is necessary. Yes, I remember Amos. And I also know of others who seem to have been compelled to preach by their sensitivity to God rather than by a burning desire. It is this fact that leads to another factor which I think is involved in one being called of God to preach.

Third, the providence of God undoubtedly plays a part in calling one to preach. Even without an overabundance of Damascus Road experiences, God still gets the attention of different ones of us through life circumstances which were not part of our own agendas. A key person's influence comes to bear. One door closes, and another opens. A family move or job transfer puts one in a situation where he is called on to use leadership and teaching skills which had never been tapped by a church. Some personal crisis humbles a man before God and causes him to reorient his life, rechannel his energy, and commit himself to unconditional service under God's direction.

Fourth, there will be opportunities for some experience in things which relate to preaching. Exposure to teaching opportunities in a church. Talks in a training class. A request to "fill in" for a preacher who is away or ill. Formal courses in public speaking or homiletics which provide training, force attempts, and give feedback. These experiences can confirm or negate a growing sense of constraint to the ministry of the gospel.

Then, fifth, I believe there will be an awareness of fulfillment and peace in the heart of someone God is calling to preach the gospel as he has experiences relevant to making that commitment. I would call it an inner confirmation to his heart by the indwelling Holy Spirit. He sees fruit come from his labor. He sees God use his efforts to bring about encounter events with Christ for people. He sees lives change through God's use of his ability to bring a word of challenge and insight from Scripture to the life of some struggling soul. If the kingdom of God really is an experience of righteousness, peace, and joy in the Holy Spirit (cf. Rom. 14:17), it cannot be unreasonable that this progression of spiritual affirmation should come to one whom God wants to be about the proclamation of the gospel.

The matter of my own conviction that God has called me to preach is consistent with this summary, and it parallels that of others who have shared their experience with me.

My personal gifts and temperament constrain me to study, to teach, to speak. I am naturally outspoken and rather gregarious as opposed to reserved. From the earliest days of my life, there has been a desire in my heart to preach. Much of this was surely due to the fact that my parents' home was always the hospitality center to preachers. Mother and Daddy respected, loved, and encouraged men who spoke the Word of God. God's providence certainly played a role in my emerging desire to preach. For example, I was a very sickly child and spent much of the first several years of my life in bed. My mother not only tutored me and nurtured an interest in books and learning generally but specifically taught me much of the content of the Word of God I still share with others. She is the best teacher of the Bible I have ever had. God worked a situation which had very little positive about it in terms of my health and the strain near-constant illness put on my family to a good end. When I was 13, James Meadows taught a training class on Sunday evenings which got a few of us on our feet to make presentations. Bruce Simpson and I were appointed by him to make short talks at a Wednesday evening service as the class ended. From that came a few more chances to preach, and at age 14 I was preaching every Lord's Day. The first and third Sundays I was inflicted on the good people at Rogers Spring, Tennessee, and on the second and fourth tormented the patient little group at Spring Hill, near Somerville, Tennessee. People such as Mathie Capshaw, U. A. Jacobs, and Sam Morris told me I was doing God's work and should give my life to preaching.

Over the years, through times of spiritual struggle, theological upheaval, and sin, God has continued to confirm the decision I have made to respond to a call he placed on my life. On the very day when I was writing this chapter, for instance, a young man stood up at an informal luncheon with some graduate students at Abilene Christian University. He began, "Five years ago, a girl from Waco wrote you about her boyfriend who wasn't a Christian and who was enamored of some philosophical writings which he thought make it impossible to believe in God . . ." He traced the story through to the boyfriend's conversion three and a half years ago. To their marriage. To the man's enrollment at Abilene to prepare himself to preach. To the identification of himself as that man. And he thanked me for writing to that girl and for encouraging her to continue her witness about Christ before him.

Am I doing what I am supposed to be doing with my life? Practically every day provides an affirmation like the one just related. The empowering presence of the Spirit of God continues to refresh my own occasionally dejected spirit with peace and joy. That God uses my sermons, my letters, my writings, or any other element of my life to bring about encounters with Christ for others is a witness to his power to show strength in weakness, to deposit treasure in clay, to be glorified in a sinner who deserves nothing but his wrath.

> In order to save many God concentrates on a few. He makes his appeal known to all through some. He sends forth his word into the hearts and minds of his chosen witnesses, who are burdened with the mystery of the divine word within them.[7]

The awareness of being called by God to preach is indispensable, especially for the prophetic elements of the preacher's work. It is the essential base on which fidelity to God can rest when a word of confrontation has to be spoken in his name. It is the actuating power for boldness and the restraint to pride. It is God who called. It is his message being spoken. It is his responsibility to produce the result. Thus any credit or honor or glory which come of the process belong to him.

A Priestly Motive

A third constituent of the total motive for preaching relates to the *priestly* dimension of the work of ministering the gospel of Christ to men, and the fitting motive for this work is personal consecration to the Lord Jesus.

I expect to meet initial resistance from some on using this term within my heritage. Yes, I know and believe Peter's statement about the church as a "royal priesthood" (1 Pet. 2:9). I accept the biblical truth that every Christian is a priest who offers up his or her own person as a living sacrifice to God in daily sanctification (Rom. 12:1). I also

---

[7]Richard Holloway, *Beyond Belief* (Grand Rapids: William B. Eerdmans, 1981), p. 28.

affirm that such activities of public worship as prayer and praise are offered from each believing heart directly to God; they are not mediated to God through the ministry of a priesthood such as ancient Israel maintained under the Law of Moses.

In spite of all this, however, I still insist on what everyone knows. Preaching is a special work which has to do with the leading of a major part of public worship. On any given Lord's Day, the sermon is an act of worship within the larger context of congregational worship. What one does with that sermon either builds or tears down, encourages or discourages, points to Christ or leaves people to their confusion. Because of our public teaching role within churches, we are not only worship leaders but theologians to their members. And, in a very real sense, these people see us as mediators of God's truth and grace to their lives.

> This ministry of the Word is not an order but an office, a function, a task to be performed. As a means of grace the ministry of the Word belongs to the whole church, the community of believers, with each believer called to bear witness to God's Word in deed and speech. This is the priesthood of believers. But a specially trained leadership is necessary. Martin Luther argued that we are all priests (lay ministers), but we are not all public ministers.[8]

Is it arrogance or impertinence to acknowledge what everyone knows to be true about our work? Why do people want to talk with us about biblical texts? Why do they ask us to pray for their hurts and problems? Why do they want us to be there for their weddings and funerals? Why do they let

---

[8]Fisher, *Who Dares to Preach?*, p. 67.

others make announcements but insist on our monopolizing the preaching and teaching times?

Scripture teaches what some of us tend to deny about the tutorial-intermediary-advocacy role of preaching. "It was [Christ] who gave some to be apostles, some to be prophets, some to be evangelists, and some to be pastors and teachers," said Paul, "to prepare God's people for works of service, so that the body of Christ may be built up until we all reach unity in the faith and in the knowledge of the Son of God and become mature, attaining the full measure of perfection found in Christ" (Eph. 4:11-13).

We are not priests in the sense of offering sacrifices of atonement for others. Jesus is the one and only High Priest to make atonement for all our sins. But we do have a priestly role in exhorting believers to offer themselves as living sacrifices to God, in equipping them for ministry in the local church, and in leading them in situations of public worship.

Perhaps "personal consecration" is not the correct or most expressive term to identify the motive here. If the prophetic element of my ministry arises from a sense of being called of God, the priestly element of it arises from my sense of being set apart for and used by God to model, to explain, to make desirable to others, and to provide opportunities for their involvement with sacred realities.

The point I am struggling to make is consistent with Peterson's lament that preachers in America "have metamorphosed into a company of shopkeepers."[9] With that metaphor he challenges the image of entrepreneurial ministry which is preoccupied with "how to keep the customers

---

[9]Eugene H. Peterson, *Working the Angles* (Grand Rapids: William B. Eerdman's Publishing Co., 1987), p. 1.

happy, how to lure customers away from competitors down the street, how to package the goods so that the customers will lay out more money."[10] Peterson is right. Some of us are getting our ministry guidelines from Lee Iacocca and Donald Trump rather than Jesus. Some of our goals relate to being the biggest and splashiest rather than biblical, spiritual, and faithful.

Our churches need more than good homileticians in their pulpits; they need good men in those pulpits who pay appropriate attention to homiletical concerns. We need fewer preachers who think of their image as religious leaders in the community; we need more who think of the spiritual welfare of the people in their congregations. We need fewer preachers flocking to church growth seminars where the tone is Harvard Business School and the technique is preacher as church administrator; we need more of us being driven to the Word in contrition, spending serious time on our knees on behalf of the people we know in our churches, and giving meaningful instruction in the gospel which will make a difference in people's lives. The difference must be real in our own lives. Christ must be transforming us daily. We must be entering deeply into the heart of God through spiritual pilgrimage. We must be learning how to make public worship vibrant rather than boring, practicing and teaching the art of personal worship, modeling and explaining how to share faith in the world, and so on.

Some men who mistakenly call themselves preachers will have to encounter Christ in their own lives, repent of their Spirit-less agendas, and reorient themselves to the deeper life of personal consecration. I make this claim

---

[10]Ibid.

against others confessionally rather than contemptuously. It is the easiest thing in the world to get so consumed with committees, projects, productivity, and brotherhood issues that the last thing one has time for is God.

It comes as a revelation to some that the concept of a kingdom of priests is not new to the New Testament. According to Exodus 19:3-6, Yahweh's intention was to make Israel into a "kingdom of priests and a holy nation." So the job of Old Testament priests was not to perfect holiness among the few. Theirs was a leadership role to exhibit holiness and to teach devotion and to draw the entire community into the meaningful experience of covenant life.

> It is not ultimately the priest who achieves the reconciliation between God and people for whom the ministry of priesthood is intended. Nor is it the priest's place to shoulder responsibility for the piety of others. The tasks are specific, discrete, and in a certain impossible sense 'manageable.' The priest may honestly rest assured that the obedient discharge of the assigned functions is sufficient. The mystery of how God may use these 'manageable' functions of priesthood to accomplish God's work of reconciliation is beyond the priest's wisdom and outside the priest's responsibility.[11]

There seems to be a great deal of insight for us in this explication of the function of Israel's priests. As worship leaders, teachers, examples, and equipping agents, preachers perform a priestly role in the lives of people under our influence. We do not use these functions to manipulate

---

[11]James A. Wharton, "Theology and Ministry in the Hebrew Scriptures," in Earl E. Shelp and Ronald Sunderland, eds., *A Biblical Basis for Ministry* (Philadelphia: Westminster Press, 1981), p. 48.

people to our agendas. We consecrate ourselves and our work to God with the confidence that his ability to make what we have done into encounters with Christ for them is sufficient. It is his mysterious work to perform. It is outside our ability or responsibility to understand.

The Pastoral Motive

The final part of the total motive for preaching which I ask you to consider is typically discussed first. It is the *pastoral* motive. I do not use the term here to indicate an office but a function, as will be made clear shortly. This is the part of a preacher's motivation that has to do with personal involvement in formal counseling and close friendship. It deals with people in times of birth and death, marriage and crisis, success and failure. And the only appropriate motivation for such involvement is love.

The general understanding today seems to be that one builds a ministry within a local church through personal, pastoral-type involvement with people which, in turn, makes his preaching credible. Recently a church indicated it would like me to help in its search for a new minister. The first qualification, the elder indicated, was that the man be a "good mixer." He went on to explain that the church was convinced that the most important thing for its preachers historically was warmth and genuineness. They would tolerate mediocre-to-poor preaching skills, he explained, for the sake of finding such a person.

My fear is that this man's explicit profile of a preacher is implicit with many who are Search Committee members or elders. And I believe it explains why there are so many weak, stunted, and lifeless churches among us.

Several years ago, I chanced to visit a church of about 200 members that was in a rural area. The inadequately prepared speaker mounted the pulpit with Leroy Brownlow's *Some Do's and Don'ts for the Christian* and proceeded to preach Chapter Four. He hadn't even bothered to copy his plagiarized outline into his own handwriting. Smoke must have been coming out my ears later as I "exposed" the man to my father. Daddy smiled, made it clear that I was revealing nothing that everyone didn't already know, but explained that the man's slothfulness in the pulpit was tolerated because everybody liked him so. He hunted, fished, and drank coffee with the best of them. The operative theory seems to have been, for this man and for a number of others like him, that "people just can't help liking him." But can that man possibly like himself? Can he think he is discharging the highest calling in the world? Being everybody's "good ole boy" may be important to a church's comfort level and help preserve the *status quo*. It will not get God's work done in the world. Genuine warmth and caring must be part of a preacher's profile, but they are not a substitute for his work of preaching.

I believe a biblical model generally begins with effective public proclamation and moves to times of private exchange, counsel, and involvement. Paul clearly considered his apostolic-evangelistic ministry primary. He was not a counselor or church-growth expert. Yet, out of his sense of compulsion for preaching the gospel, he also has a pastoral heart for the churches he founded and the believers he taught. "I face daily the pressure of my concern for all the churches," he wrote. "Who is weak, and I do not feel weak? Who is led into sin, and I do not inwardly burn?" (2 Cor. 11:28-29). This concern in his life was but the natural expression of his understanding of the church as Christ's spiritual body: "If one part suffers, every part suffers with it;

if one part is honored, every part rejoices with it" (1 Cor. 12:26).

I understand the office of bishop, presbyter, elder, and pastor to be one and the same (cf. 1 Tim. 3:1; Tit. 1:5, 7; Eph. 4:11). But while the *office* of bishop or pastor is reserved to those individuals who are appointed to it in light of the qualifications given in 1 Timothy 3 and Titus 1, I do not understand that these are the only people who cultivate a pastoral heart toward other people. Older brothers and sisters must have such a heart toward younger ones, teachers for their students, and preachers for all our hearers.

If one preaches out of the personal motivation of gratitude for grace received, speaks prophetically from a sense of being called of God to his work, functions in a priestly role out of personal consecration to the Lord, he will have people seeking him out for personal instruction, counsel, prayer, and guidance. Whether he is prepared for those times will depend not only on his formal training for ministry but even more on his love for the people he serves.

Willimon refers to a survey he did among some rural churches in North Carolina. He was seeking a definition of "good preaching." The characteristic which surfaced again and again was this that good preachers *"preach as if they were preaching to individual listeners and their problems."*[12] I suspect the result of his unscientific poll about good preaching would extrapolate well into other states and over people from other religious traditions. I also think you can put it down as an indicator of the effectiveness of your own preaching that you are serving people well when they say over and over: "You must have been reading my mind or

---

[12]Willimon, *Integrative Preaching*, p. 15. Italics in original.

eavesdropping on my conversations this week to have preached that sermon today!"

When people affirm to you that your sermons are addressing their lives directly and making a meaningful difference, you can be sure that the Holy Spirit is involved in the process. He is convicting hearts through the preached Word. He is linking preacher and hearer in a heart-to-heart relationship. Christ is being encountered in those sermons! And people will come to your door and ring your phone and ask you to their homes. They will want to explore specific implications of the Word of God to their lives with you.

Question: Are you capable of the love which will be required to follow through with them?

Don't sacrifice your set times for prayer, study, and preparation. But once your sermons have begun to have divine power in their delivery, you must be prepared to give of yourself at a personal level for the people who have heard God's Word through you.

> Phillips Brooks once said that he never sat down to write a sermon without thinking of the calls that should be made, nor did he ever go out calling without thinking of the sermon waiting to be written. We may as well make up our minds to live with that tension. There is no resolution of it.[13]

The reason some preachers can do well on short-term preaching endeavors or in mission settings is that, for brief periods of time, they are willing to let people "wear them out" in engaging the Word of God with their lives. That is the ongoing pastoral task in preaching. It does not

---

[13]Bartlett, *The Audacity of Preaching*, p. 138.

mean that you must be Superman. It does not give you the arrogant right to assume that you are indispensable, that you have the privilege of neglecting your family for the sake of others, or that you cannot afford to take time to rest and energize yourself against the constant demands that are being made. But it does mean that you will work hard. Very hard. And the hardest thing about this part of your work will be the struggling in prayer on behalf of the people, situations, and crises you see.

Conclusion

The motive for preaching, then, is not a single one. Preaching itself is not a narrow and neat work. If it is an event of encounter between the Living Christ and people seeking after God, it will demand many, many things of us. As a multi-faceted work, it partakes of a multi-faceted motivation.

Because of our differences of temperament, some will find their greatest compulsion to ministry in the pastoral motive of love for hurting, lost people. Others will be best at the priestly work of worship, teaching, and equipping others out of their own personal consecration. Still others will function most effectively for the Lord in a priestly role because of their strong sense of having received a divine call. Surely all of us who preach must sense daily the personal motivation of gratitude for divine grace which undergirds not only what we do but who we are before God.

May God deliver us from the impure and mixed motives with which we sometimes serve him. And may we nurture, deepen, and purify the motives which are holy to our calling so he can be glorified through the preaching of the gospel by such unworthy yet willing servants as ourselves.

The Message

Introduction

What is the *message* we preach? We are not politicians or sociologists. We are neither program administrators nor moralists. Our calling is not to be either a flamethrower for God or a balm to guilty consciences. God has called us to challenge men and women to encounter Jesus Christ in his role as Savior and Lord. "For I resolved to know nothing while I was with you except Jesus Christ and him crucified," wrote Paul to disciples at Corinth (1 Cor. 2:2; cf. 1:17, 23). Can we say the same of our ministries? If not, they are unfaithful ministries.

In this lecture, my appeal is for us to adopt a Pauline single-mindedness about the content of our preaching. The cross is *the* issue of the Christian religion. Jesus Christ and him crucified is the one and only theme for us to preach. Everything we are about must find its meaning in terms of Calvary; anything whose significance is defined in terms other than the cross of our Lord is a distraction from our calling.

This is not to say that preaching should become so narrow in its focus that the only biblical texts we expound from the pulpit are passion narratives or that we simply say over and over again that Christ died for our sins according to the Scriptures, that he was buried, and that he was raised on the third day. It is to say that we must show how all our needs are met by the cross. We must teach people how the cross informs values, determines commitments, and motivates holiness. As we go about our special work in local churches, it is our role to help people relate everything the church is about to Christ's atonement.

> But for preaching to be truly Christian, however narrow or specific the truth that is enforced in any one sermon, both preacher and people must set this specific truth in the broad context of redemption and view it from the standpoint which would have prevailed if its relation to the Deed of redemption were set forth.[1]

Some churches have lost their reason for being. Thus they are casting about for a mandate. On reflection, however, "mandate" may be too strong a word. Some appear willing to accept any rallying cry or church-growth gimmick that promises to keep the doors open and pay the bills. This approach often degenerates into massaging egos rather than preaching Christ. The tragedy, scandal, and offense of the cross are abandoned. This is what I take to be the central point made by Allen, Hughes, and Weed in their analysis of the church at the end of the twentieth century.

> By the waning years of the twentieth century, many American churches seemed more concerned to save

---

[1]Miller, *Fire in Thy Mouth*, p. 149.

> marriages than souls, more interested in self-esteem
> than salvation, and more concerned to relieve de-
> pression and anxiety than to deal with the fundamen-
> tal reality of sin.[2]

What they call the "secularization" of American Christianity parallels an abandonment of the cross as its focus for preaching. Abandon Christ and him crucified as the burden of our preaching and all that remains is to model the church on a business model. Survey the market, appraise the latest fads, and pick what you hope will be a "hot seller" in a consumer-oriented church.

The church does not exist to console sinners, but to save them. Its mission is not to help Christians "find themselves," but to challenge them to lose their lives for Christ's sake. Its goal must not become "success" measured by the world's criteria of numbers, building, and money, but to be faithful to Christ.

A church has four primary responsibilities, and the fulfillment of each of them requires that the preaching done among its people revolve around the cross as its hub. The church exists in visible, incarnational form to exhibit God's glory, power, and righteousness to the world and to reach beyond itself in order to carry the knowledge of salvation to people facing eternity without Christ. Each of these tasks relates directly to the cross and its significance to the people of God.

The Glory of God

The church is called to *exhibit God's glory to the world in joyous, celebrational worship.*

---

[2]C. Leonard Allen, Richard T. Hughes, and Michael R. Weed, *The Worldly Church* (Abilene, TX: ACU Press, 1988), pp. 30-31.

Worship is an important experience in the Christian life. It bonds the church together as a family of believers. It affirms identity. It makes a statement to the watching world. Yet the bond can become an uneasy truce, the identity a sectarian disposition, and the statement a vague anthology of boring platitudes.

Many Christians are expressing their dismay with the worship experience they find in our churches. They use words like "boring" and "lifeless" to describe it. They don't sense anything meaningful happening on a regular basis. A handful of songs is sung over and over. Communion is rushed. And sermons are either dull academic lectures on some textual point which is not applied to life or else amateur comedy routines which leave one starving for a word from God. So more and more of our members, especially the younger ones, are visiting other churches.

Not many who grew up in other fellowships or who have no church background whatever are impressed with or attracted by our worship. It seems stale to them. Not because there are no brass bands or choruses but because it seems so routine, predictable, and joyless. They don't sense a spirit of excitement and celebration which would cause them to want to know its source.

Christians have something to celebrate, and our worship should affirm and identify it. If we take as our cue the vision of Christ in Revelation 5, we may worship him as the living creatures and elders in heaven did by singing:

> You are worthy . . .
> because you were slain,
>> and with your blood you purchased men for
>> God

> from every tribe and language and people
> and nation.
> You have made them to be a
> kingdom and priests to serve our God,
> and they will reign on the earth (Rev. 5:9-10).

The etymology of our English word "worship" traces back to the Anglo-Saxon *weorthscipe*, later *worthship*. To worship God, whether Father, Son, Holy Spirit, or the full Godhead, is to assign supreme worth. If we ascribe such a position to the Lord Jesus Christ, it is on the basis of his redemptive work. In keeping with a passover-theology motif, John presents Christ as praiseworthy because of his death and the purchase of men for God with his own blood. In our worship, the same theme of praise is to be sounded. The church, the community of the cross, celebrates the victory won by our Savior in his death, burial, and resurrection. There is no excuse for allowing what is supposed to be a joyous celebration degenerate into a tiresome ritual.

In his Corinthian correspondence, Paul tied the church's worship directly to the cross. In contrasting "the Lord's table" with "the table of demons" (1 Cor. 10:21), the table metaphor probably stands for the total worship experience and not just the Lord's Supper. In either case, he refers to the communion specifically by asking, "Is not the cup of thanksgiving for which we give thanks a participation in the blood of Christ?" (1 Cor. 10:16a). The wine taken in the Lord's Supper is a cup for which we give thanks, a cup over which we have pronounced thanksgiving, a cup which elicits the thanksgiving of all who drink of it. It reminds us that our sin debt was paid, not with the blood of bulls and goats, but with the precious blood of God's own son. It reminds us that our sins have been washed away by that blood.

"And is not the bread that we break a participation in the body of Christ?" Paul continued. "Because there is one loaf, we, who are many, are one body, for we all partake of the one loaf" (1 Cor. 10:16b-17). Any ceremonial sharing in that which had been sacrificed, whether among Jews or pagans, meant that the person became a participant in the sacrificial act. Thus, in eating the one loaf together, the church affirms anew the reconciliation with God which has been effected through the cross and its reconciliation among all who are partaking of the single loaf as one body in Christ.

Among its own members, the Lord's Supper is a reminder that our hope rests entirely on the death, burial, and resurrection of Jesus (1 Cor. 11:23-25). To outsiders who may be present to witness it, it is a proclamation of the Lord's death until he returns (1 Cor. 11:26).

Only if the cross is deliberately kept at the center of the worship experience will worship be saved from boredom, formality, and trivialization. Only then will it be celebrational in nature.

The Power of God

The church also exists to *demonstrate the transforming power of God in the world.*

Salvation is a personal and individual matter. One is not saved through his presence with or even membership in a church; salvation is a personal participation in the death, burial, and resurrection of Christ (cf. Gal. 2:20; Rom. 6:3-4). On the other hand, one may still be saved -- though surely with greater difficulty -- though he is a member of an unfaithful church; "a few people" in Sardis were destined to walk with Christ in spite of the church's general apostasy (Rev. 3:4).

Nevertheless, though salvation is both personal and individual, it is *not private*. One who is born anew by the water and Spirit is simultaneously born into the family of God. He or she becomes a brother or sister to all others who have been spiritually reborn and becomes part of a community of faith. Thus the New Testament represents the Christian as a member of a larger family (Eph. 2:19), a citizen within a new race or nation (1 Pet. 2:9), a building block within the Lord's holy temple (Eph. 2:21), and a part of the body of Christ (1 Cor. 12:27).

> Thus the very purpose of his self-giving on the cross was not just to save isolated individuals, and so perpetuate their loneliness, but to create a new community whose members would belong to him, love one another, and eagerly serve the world.[3]

Within the new community of the cross, something astonishing happens. The old, sinful nature of a believer is replaced by a new, holy character. The works of the flesh give way to the fruit of the Spirit. God's power to make that person into a new creation exhibits itself. We typically refer to this total process as the edification of the church. How does it happen?

The *human method* for bringing about change is power exerted through moralism and legalism. It is basically a self-help approach rooted in the maxim "I must try harder." It spins out rules, systems, and methodologies. It believes that by trying hard enough we can make ourselves better.

---

[3]John R. W. Stott, *The Cross of Christ* (Downers Grove, IL: InterVarsity Press, 1986), p. 255.

This method is unquestionably rooted in pride and insists on our ability to control our own lives and destinies.

The *divine method* for producing change is power through surrender. It is paradoxical and antithetical to pride. Beginning in the fact of the atonement provided through Christ's act of surrender to evil men, unjust acts, and death, we are asked to believe that his death was our death.

My status as a lawbreaker demands that I suffer the death penalty, but to suffer it means to be separated from God in hell forever and leaves me utterly without hope. So Christ took my deserved penalty when he surrendered to an undeserved death on the cross. Now that I trust his death as payment of my penalty, now that I am one with him, now that I have been baptized into his death -- "I have been crucified with Christ and I no longer live, but Christ lives in me" (Gal. 2:20a).

To be "in Christ" is to be so united with him that all his experiences become our experiences. His death for sin was our own death, so our lawbreaking and condemned selves have died. Yet, in another sense, we are still living. But now it is Christ's life we are experiencing. Just as he was raised from the dead and ascended to the Father, so we have been "raised up with Christ and seated with him in the heavenly realms in Christ Jesus" (Eph. 2:6).

Growing out of this crucifixion with Christ, we are now called to crucify the lusts of our flesh which originally led to our condemnation as lawbreakers. More than that, we are given power from God to do so. Paul wrote: "Those who belong to Christ Jesus have crucified the sinful nature with its passions and desires" (Gal. 5:24). Is this simply an advanced form of moralism? Is Paul slipping back into his Jewish legalism? Not at all. "Since we live by the Spirit," he continued, "let us keep in step with the Spirit" (Gal. 5:25).

Surrendering in faith to Christ's death in our place redeems us from the past, and surrendering in faith to the resident power of the Holy Spirit enables us for the present.

As Stott points out, the two crucifixions of Galatians 2:20 and 5:24 are distinct events.

> The first speaks of our freedom from the condemnation of the law by sharing in *Christ's* crucifixion, the second of our freedom from the power of the flesh by ensuring *its* crucifixion. These two, namely to have been crucified with Christ (passive) and to have crucified the flesh (active), must not be confused.[4]

Though distinct, however, these two crucifixions are not unrelated. The latter is possible only because of the former, and both are victories to grace alone. The only source of power to transform human minds, hearts, and lives is with God.

Within the community where this power is being exerted, something happens that cannot happen in the world. Barriers of sex, race, and economics become irrelevant. Lies give way to truth, and hatred is replaced by love. Righteousness is more important than profit or prominence. Narcissistic self-gratification, with fidelity to individual feelings as the final test of authenticity, is replaced by committed discipleship.

The defining and unifying factor in this whole process is the cross. It grounds faith and rallies good works in the name of Christ. It alone accounts for a radical new view of reality which allows the church to be the church: a community, people growing in biblical understanding, saints discov-

---

[4]Stott, *Cross of Christ*, p. 349.

ering their gifts from God, and workers functioning for the sake of God's kingdom among men.

> The cross is not a sign of the church's quiet, suffering submission to the powers-that-be, but rather the church's revolutionary participation in the victory of Christ over those powers. The cross is not a symbol for general human suffering and oppression. Rather, the cross is a sign of what happens when one takes God's account of reality more seriously than Caesar's. The cross stands as God's (and our) eternal no to the powers of death, as well as God's eternal yes to humanity, God's remarkable determination not to leave us to our own devices.[5]

The failure we lament as a lack of spirituality and commitment in churches is rooted in a much more fundamental failure to preach the cross as the church's *raison d'etre*. No, it is surely a theological shallowness which has not yet understood the cross as our heart and essence. We have been *a*-theological in our past and have been content to live as dogmatists, proof-texters, and polemicists. Preaching has tended to focus on a list of "issues" rather than on the cross and its meaning.

This lack of preaching about the true meaning of the cross has resulted in nominal commitment. The substitution of pop psychology for Christ's cross has created an embarrassing tolerance for sin among those who hear such preaching. The God presented as transcendent, holy, and challenging by the prophets has become an affable chum concerned with enhancing humanity's self-esteem. The cross has been replaced by the couch -- for people discerning enough to

[5]Stanley Hauerwas and William H. Willimon, *Resident Aliens* (Nashville: Abingdon Press, 1989), p. 47.

know they need to change, the psychiatrist's couch; for those oblivious to their need for change, the couch in front of the TV.

Jesus spoke of cross-bearing as the vocation of every disciple (cf. Luke 9:23). Only one cross serves a redemptive purpose in the divine plan, but every follower of the one who died on it must bear his own cross. Understood biblically, the cross always signifies someone's death.

When someone in the first-century world started down the road with a cross, everyone knew he would not return. It was the end for him. He said goodbye to everything he had known or been. When the work of his cross was done, he would be gone.

This significance of the cross is why it is the symbol of Christianity. The old man does not need a new perspective. The sinful nature does not need a new and passionate commitment. That person needs to be destroyed. Done away with once and for all. Terminated! Since God is holy and cannot compromise with sin, the only way he can save a sinner is to destroy him and then raise him to newness of life. Salvation is less God's act of putting a new suit on an old man or woman than it is his putting a new person in the suit. This is Paul's meaning at Galatians 2:20. This is the process he surveyed in Romans 6:1ff.

Yet we hear people talk of a rebellious son or arthritis as "my cross to bear." Life's common troubles are not the crosses Christians bear. Has our preaching so minimized the cross that people understand it so?

Bonhoeffer was correct in saying that a disciple's role in taking up the cross is an event of self-denial which carries implications for a specifically Christian life.

> If our Christianity has ceased to be serious about discipleship, if we have watered down the gospel into emotional uplift which makes no costly demands and which fails to distinguish between natural and Christian existence, then we cannot help regarding the cross as an ordinary everyday calamity, as one of the trials and tribulations of life. We have then forgotten that the cross means rejection and shame as well as suffering. The Psalmist was lamenting that he was despised and rejected of men, and that is an essential quality of the suffering of the cross. But this notion has ceased to be intelligible to a Christianity which can no longer see any difference between an ordinary human life and a life committed to Christ.[6]

The cross, then, is at the heart of discipleship. There can be no new life with Christ apart from sharing his experience of the cross, both passively and actively. "When Christ calls a man, he bids him come and die."[7] That we have so many church members who are dunked but not dead argues that we have been sidetracked from preaching the cross.

Fellowship, edification, and evangelism happen in the church. But they are not the outcome of well-administered programs. They are by-products of the project of preaching Christ and him crucified.

Social Justice

The church exists to *display God's righteousness within a fallen, hostile environment.*

Christians are people holding dual citizenship. Whether citizens of first-century Rome, eighteenth-century

---

[6]Dietrich Bonhoeffer, *The Cost of Discipleship*, revised and unabridged ed., trans. R. H. Fuller and Irmgard Booth (New York: Macmillan, 1963), p. 98.

[7]Ibid., p. 99.

France, or twentieth-century America, we are nevertheless aware that "our citizenship is in heaven" (Phil. 3:20a). Yet the fact remains that, although committed to the priority of our heavenly citizenship, we also still hold earthly citizenship. How are we to integrate our dual responsibilities? More particularly, what is the relationship between a disciple's obligation to be separate from the world and his duty to minister to its victims?

With his famous salt and light metaphors (Matt. 5:13-16), Jesus gave some essential insights to guide us in this matter. First, Christians are called to be as different from non-Christians in values and behavior as salt is from rot, light from dark, or -- as we would more likely put it -- oil from water. Second, though called to be spiritually distinct from non-Christians, believers are to penetrate society as salt penetrates meat. Third, the church is a visible counter-culture where Christians keep promises, treat the poor with respect, love our enemies, and otherwise serve as lightbearers to people on the outside. Fourth, losing our distinctiveness from the world makes us useless to Christ in a non-Christian society.

Following Christ's example, we are not called to monasticism but to *sacred secularity*. That is, we are to live in earthly community with a heavenly commitment. We are to serve God by serving the community, and we are to serve the community by exhibiting and declaring the values we know in Christ.

Jesus did not isolate himself from people to the degree that John the Baptist had before him. If John was a man of desert asceticism, Jesus was a man of city sociability. He moved among people. He taught large crowds. He was available for private interviews. In every setting, he demonstrated compassion for confused, sick, or exploited people. Early in his ministry, he was asked to read Scripture in the Nazareth synagogue. He read a text from Isaiah 61 which speaks of blessing poor people, prisoners, blind persons, and the oppressed. After reading it aloud, he said, "Today this scripture is fulfilled in your hearing" (Luke 4:18-19).

Throughout his ministry, Jesus associated with outcasts and the poor. He healed the sick, blind, and lame. He paid attention to children and women. By both his words about them and his actions with them, Jesus proclaimed that God's mercy reached to these classes of people that were systematically excluded by the religious establishment of his time.[8]

Following Jesus' example, a faithful church will influence its culture in significant and obvious ways. That greed, sexual immorality, drugs, racism, and divorce are routine in our culture does not need proof. That this is so in a country where 94 percent say they believe in God and one-third claim to have had a life-changing religious experience[9] indicts us for unfaithfulness. That much salt and light *should* make a detectable difference.

Here are some of the issues before our world today: peace, racism, crime, homelessness, child abuse, chemical dependency, materialism, ethics in government, AIDS, teen pregnancy, gambling, abortion, pornography. Which of these is unworthy of our concern? Our prayers? Our involvement?

---

[8]Cf. Joachim Jeremias, *New Testament Theology*, trans. John Bowden (New York: Charles Scribner's Sons, 1971), pp. 108-121, for a summary of Gospel texts on this issue and their literary background.

[9]"Survey finds 94% say they believe in God," *The* (Nashville) *Tennessean*, Nov. 26, 1989, p. B6

Two equally fatal errors compromise the integrity of the religion of Jesus Christ. On the one hand, some Christians are so concerned about the world to come that they are no earthly good. On the other hand, some get so caught up in this world that they forget to keep their focus on a goal which lies outside this world. The real challenge is for the church to live heavenly truth so faithfully that it makes a worldly difference.

It is the preaching of the cross that brings about such a result. For one thing, that Jesus died for such persons means that they cannot be unimportant to or unloved by God; thus we cannot turn our backs on them. For another, the crucifixion of our old beings removes the pride that could otherwise keep us from poor, imprisoned, or "unworthy" people. Finally, there is Christ's word for it that anything done "for one of the least of these brothers of mine" is regarded as an act of service to him (Matt. 25:40).

> Being a minister . . . is not a vocation merely to help people. We are called to help people "in the name of Jesus." And that's the rub. In fact, we are *not* called to help people. We are called to follow Jesus, in whose service we find out who we are and how to help and be helped. . . . His is an ethic built not upon helping people or even upon results, certainly not upon helping folk to be a bit better adjusted within an occupied Judea. His actions are based upon his account of how God is "kind to the ungrateful and the selfish," making the sun to rise on the good and the bad. We are called to "be perfect" even as our Heavenly Father is.[10]

[10]Hauerwas and Willimon, *Resident Aliens*, p. 121.

On the one hand, then, a Christian stands over against his culture as a light shining into the darkness, and the church exists as a city set on a hill. The searching soul can move in the direction of that light and see the cross as its ultimate source of radiance. On the other hand, the community of the cross infiltrates the world as salt and becomes its conscience. In this case, an uneasiness with evil initiates a search which can only be satisfied by the crucified Son of God.

Evangelistic Outreach

The church exists to reach beyond itself to *bring the lost to a saving knowledge of Jesus Christ.*

It is at this point that preaching reaches its crescendo. It is here that the attractiveness of worship, the credibility of discipleship, and the compassion of social justice coalesce to focus the sinner's attention on the word that can bring him life. Our task in preaching is to enable people to grasp the wonderful love of God for sinners which is shown on the cross.

When we preach evangelistically, we must preach boldly and prophetically. Yet we must preach with such tender concern for the lost that Christ's own love which took him to the cross is seen in our faces and heard in our voices. We must make it clear that we are not preaching a system, a creed, or a series of steps. We are preaching Christ. And our preaching must also have a greater goal than arousing curiosity or proving a point. We are offering a relationship. As though God himself were making the appeal through us, we preach to implore men and women to be reconciled to God through Jesus Christ (cf. 2 Cor. 5:20).

The late A. W. Tozer had this to say of preaching the cross:

> We who preach the gospel must not think of
> ourselves as public relations agents sent to establish
> good will between Christ and the world. We must not
> imagine ourselves commissioned to make Christ
> acceptable to big business, the press, the world of
> sports or modern education. We are not diplomats
> but prophets, and our message is not a compromise
> but an ultimatum.
>
> God offers life, but not an improved old life.
> The life He offers is life out of death. It stands always
> on the far side of the cross. Whoever would possess
> it must pass under the rod. He must repudiate himself
> and concur in God's just sentence against him.[11]

Our preaching of the cross must help people understand such concepts as vicarious suffering and substitutionary atonement. Though we may never use these "heavy"
theological terms in our sermons, we must paint the picture
of Calvary so vividly before them that they see Jesus dying.
Dying in their place. Dying in order to give them life.

In the summer of 1988, my 17-year-old son and I were
in Poland for several days. During the time we were there,
we made special arrangements to take an express train from
Warsaw to Krakow. From there we went by car to the
infamous Nazi concentration camp named Auschwitz. From
the records and artifacts preserved there, I am convinced
that the hundreds of thousands who had to endure its
horrors came as close to hell on Earth as a human can get.
While we were there, I told him the story and together we
retraced the steps of Maximilian Kolbe.

Kolbe was arrested by the Gestapo and interred at
Auschwitz in February of 1941 for "political crimes." A

---

[11]A. W. Tozer, *Man: The Dwelling Place of God* (Harrisburg,
PA: Christian Publications, Inc., 1966), pp. 44-45.

Franciscan priest, he had been helping Jewish refugees escape from Poland.

Toward the end of July in that same year, an escape was discovered in Kolbe's section of the prison during roll call. An SS officer arbitrarily selected ten men to die by starvation in reprisal. At the reading of one man's name, Francizek Gajowniczek, the condemned sergeant in the Polish Army cried out, "Have mercy! I have a wife and children!"

Prisoner 16670 broke ranks at that point and offered to take Gajowniczek's place. His name was not on the list of ten. He was not under a death sentence. "I am a priest," Maximilian Kolbe said. "I have no family." For reasons we will never know, the officer in charge allowed the exchange. The condemned man, unable even to thank the man who was taking his place, stepped back into line. The uncondemned volunteer who was taking his place was led to a basement cell with nine other men, stripped of his clothes, and left to die of starvation and exposure.

The 47-year-old Kolbe survived for approximately two weeks without food or water. He died on August 14, when a prison guard put him out of his misery with an injection of phenol into his heart.

The Kolbe-Gajowniczek story is a microcosm of the gospel story. Jesus died so I could be spared. His fellowship with the Father and Holy Spirit was broken on the cross for the only time in his eternal existence. He tasted hell for me that day! "This is how we know what love is: Jesus Christ laid down his life for us" (1 John 3:16).

My name was on the list of the damned. And so was yours. The wages of sin is death, and you and I are sinners. But the name of Jesus was nowhere on that list. Though he was tempted as we are, he did not sin. He did not come under condemnation. There was no death penalty due him.

When my name was called, he stepped forward. My guilt was imputed to him. Through faith, his righteousness has now been imputed to me. Undeserved love triumphed over deserved wrath in a once-for-all event of divine self-sacrifice. An unthinkable act of substitution overcame the irrevocable tension between justice and mercy. Now we have eternal life in Christ. "God made him who had no sin to be sin for us, so that in him we might become the righteousness of God" (2 Cor. 5:21).

> The concept of substitution may be said, then, to lie at the heart of both sin and salvation. For the essence of sin is man substituting himself for God, while the essence of salvation is God substituting himself for man. Man asserts himself against God and puts himself where only God deserves to be; God sacrifices himself for man and puts himself where only man deserves to be. Man claims prerogatives which belong to God alone; God accepts penalties which belong to man alone.[12]

To preach the gospel is to preach "that Christ died for our sins according to the Scriptures, that he was buried, that he was raised on the third day according to the Scriptures" (1 Cor. 15:3-4). It is to invite men and women to confess and claim the crucified Christ for themselves. With their mouths. In the beautiful symbol of baptism. And through a life of single-minded devotion to him.

Until we have learned to preach the cross, we have nothing critical to say from our pulpits. Well-crafted talks,

[12]Stott, *The Cross of Christ*, p. 160.

memorized poems, and "nice speeches" are unworthy of our mission. The pulpit is the place for the message of Christ and him crucified to be sounded forth. "The real presence of Christ crucified is what makes preaching," insists Forsyth. "It is what makes of a speech a sermon, and of a sermon Gospel."[13]

Conclusion

As a preacher addressing preachers, I think it is important for you to know a bit more about the incident related above. What became of Franciszek Gajowniczek after the horrific exchange at Auschwitz? One writer relates the reaction to his deliverance from death this way:

> The sergeant, after the initial shock of relief when Kolbe's offer is accepted, will fall into an almost suicidal depression over Kolbe's having died for him. Then, one, day, he suddenly sees himself as a man with a mission: To survive so word of the Franciscan's free-will offering of his life for a fellow human being will survive, too, to enrich the human family.[14]

The man for whom Kolbe died survived Auschwitz. He rejoined his wife and children. He erected a granite marker to the memory of the man who died in his place in the back yard of his home. He lives with the knowledge that his life since 1941 has been a gift secured by another's death. He visits Auschwitz on August 14 every year. And he has seen himself as a "man with a mission." Telling the story of Kolbe. Letting others know of a deed which gave him life.

---

[13]Forsyth, *Positive Preaching*, p. 82.
[14]Patricia Treece, *A Man for Others* (Huntington, IN: Our Sunday Visitor, Inc., 1982), p. viii.

If the Kolbe-Gajowniczek story is a miniature of the gospel, the Gajowniczek "mission" is a microcosm of preaching. We have one story to tell. Living by virtue of his death, we tell the story of his saving work with eagerness. Our very lives are monuments to him. Our hearts are filled with thoughts of him, and our lips speak of him constantly.

The Method

Introduction

Of all the section titles for these studies in preaching, this one may be the most misleading. When I speak of *method* in preaching, I cannot speak for long and can speak with no confidence whatever about homiletical technique. I am not trained in homiletics, having had one undergraduate course and one graduate course in the subject matter. My own preaching style is distinctive, if not maddening. It seldom admits of neat outlining. A friend of mine who is well-versed in homiletics despairs of fitting my homiletical method into any category known to the systematizers.

So I would not think of trying to teach homiletics. This lecture is not about homiletical method, except in the broadest possible sense. It is about method appropriate to the four elements of preaching which were set forth earlier in these investigations: personal, prophetic, priestly, and pastoral.

Come to think of it, that I do not have a homiletical method to promote could well be an advantage to this project. Since I doubt there is any one homiletical route which is either superior to all others or foolproof for the singular purpose of preaching (i.e., creating encounters wherein people stand before the Living Word), the approach I intend to take to discussing method may be used in relation to any homiletical technique you prefer.

Medicine and law are honorable professions. So are highway construction and farming. And publishing, school administration, writing, music, and a host of other careers. But there is one work to which some people are gifted, called, and consecrated which is most directly in imitation of Jesus Christ. Preaching is an attempt to follow Jesus not only in *the doing of God's will*, as every Christian does, but also in *the public proclamation of God's will*. We are servants in our ministry, and, even if we succeed -- by divine rather than mere human criteria of success -- in fulfilling it, we will have only done our duty (cf. Luke 17:7-10). The glory and the praise and the honor go to the One who called us to preach.

One of the most astounding passages in the New Testament related to our work is this: "All this is from God, who reconciled us to himself through Christ and gave us the ministry of reconciliation: that God was reconciling the world to himself in Christ, not counting men's sins against them. And he has committed to us the message of reconciliation. We are therefore Christ's ambassadors, as though God were making his appeal through us. We implore you on Christ's behalf: Be reconciled to God" (2 Cor. 5:18-20). Although most directly a comment about apostolic ministry, this text has straightforward implications for the ministry of preaching generally. When, in verse 18, Paul insists that God has "committed to *us* the ministry of reconciliation," the referent for "us" must be seen as taking in not only the apostles but their assistants and spiritual progeny -- their

Timothys and other "sons in the faith" (cf. 1 Tim. 1:2a; Tit. 1:4a). There is a sense, then, in which every gospel preacher is Christ's ambassador who participates in the ministry of reconciliation.

Dangerous Roman provinces were administered by a minister from the emperor himself. His title would be "ambassador" (Gk, *presbeutes*). His task would be to represent the interests of the emperor, to speak for the emperor, and to uphold his emperor's name. Similarly, ambassadors for Christ are always living in a foreign land and speaking for the heavenly country where their citizenship lies. They represent the interests of Christ, speak for Christ, and uphold Christ's name. Thus, while a servant, a preacher is a servant with a daring and outrageous mission. We come full circle to the sense of presumption. Audacity. Folly! How dare we allege to speak for Christ!

Holy Scripture is our source of revelation and authority. Our boldness is not from ourselves but from the authoritative Word of God. For us to affirm "The Bible says . . ." is therefore equivalent in principle to the Old Testament formula "Thus says the Lord . . . ."

For us to have such boldness from a source other than personal arrogance, we must be rooted in the Word of God. We must be responsible stewards of the divine message. We must be serious students and faithful proclaimers of a message which we know *is not* our own in origin but which *is* our own through understanding, obedience, and verbalization.

The Personal Element

The essence of the personal element in preaching method has already been anticipated in the first lecture in this series. The word *integrity* must be repeated here. As with no other person executing an assigned task, a preacher has no right to speak of something which he has not experienced. We are not actors, salesmen, or artists. We are conduits for the presence of Christ through the preached gospel. We do not have to discover or create a theme, story line, or sales pitch. We are obliged to be instruments of God's Word.

> Dependence on God then is a distinctive mark of biblical preaching. God's messengers do not preach on their own, because the life they live is not their own. Paul put it this way: 'Yet not I live, but Christ lives in me.' Christian preaching is the work of the Holy Spirit through the Word discerned by a particular man or woman who, in response to God's call, prepares and proclaims it to persons-in-community to nurture their faith and empower them to serve God in the world. Biblical preachers are channels of the Word. They are Christ's ambassadors. They give what they have first received.[1]

The focus of gospel preaching is always and ever the same. "For we do not preach ourselves," declared Paul, "but Jesus Christ as Lord, and ourselves as your servants for Jesus' sake" (2 Cor. 4:5). Our message is the one already discussed. God's love through Christ. Amazing grace. Redemption through his blood. Our role as preachers is to serve men and women by the faithful proclamation of the gospel. The truth. The whole truth. Nothing but the truth.

Since this is the case, preachers must be concerned about hermeneutics before homiletics. We must be serious about the content of the Word of God before we pursue the

---

[1]Fisher, *Who Dares to Preach?*, p. 123.

fine art of persuasion. To what shall we persuade men? To law or to grace? To husk or to kernel? To propositions or to person? To system or to relationship?

If one's academic training is in speech or family therapy or philosophy, he must resist the temptation to use the pulpit in service to his scholarly discipline. The pulpit serves Jesus Christ. It is the place for the proclamation of Good News rather than considered opinions. It exists so people can meet the Son of God rather than be swept away with rhetoric and argument.

Preaching in our tradition has too often been crippled by our deficient approach to Scripture itself. The Bible is not a spiritual haystack concealing occasional needles of propositional truth which make weighty premises for well-structured syllogisms.

Preaching in our tradition has tended to be topical. So we have preached about the two covenants, baptism, worship, abortion, and translations of the Bible. Now all these are important topics, and each deserves to be treated in some way and in an appropriate setting. But our penchant for going at them topically and with a system of proof-texting has gotten us into all sorts of trouble. And we have often missed the *real* issue of many of the texts we have used within this scheme.

Preaching in our tradition has been highly subjective while boasting of its biblical objectivity. The homiletical method I was taught had three steps: (1) Identify the point you wish to make, (2) establish your point with the Bible, and (3) illustrate that point to make it clear to your audience. As I used that method, I thought I was preaching the Bible. I was only *exploiting* (i.e., misusing, manipulating) the Bible for my own purposes.

Preaching in our tradition has sometimes been more interested in preserving our tradition than in discovering the truth. The homiletical method I have just outlined illustrates my very serious charge. Current fears being expressed by some about the concern many of us have to apply a more responsible hermeneutic to Scripture reflect the same point of view.

The hermeneutic of command, example, and inference virtually demands topical preaching. It seems to assume that historical precedent is binding unless a good reason can be given to the contrary. Mere historical precedent is *never* binding. Foot-washing, for example, we have generally refused to bind as a religious practice and have looked at those who do bind it as eccentrics. In order for a precedent/example to be "binding," there must be a theological grounding for it which is trans-cultural, timeless, and tied to the nature of God as revealed in Christ. We have tended to understand this through an intuition rather than having articulated it well in a hermeneutical system. Furthermore, the leveling of the biblical landscape by the system of command, example, and inference has tended to allow us to string together the commands of the Word of God in scissors-and-paste fashion. Even if one tries to preach progressively through a book of the Bible with this hermeneutical base, he tends to wind up identifying a theme or central thought in his handful of verses, pulling in a few other verses on that same issue, and producing a topical sermon.

Bible study which proceeds from a deliberate application of a Christocentric critical-historical procedure not only allows but practically demands expository preaching. This combination of hermeneutical method and expository preaching yields rich balance in preaching, keeps preaching from becoming a flight of fancy, and teaches both us and our hearers to ask the right question of the text (i.e., What did the writer intend these words to mean?).

> At heart, expository preaching is not just a method but a commitment, a view of the essence of preaching, a homiletical approach to preach the Scriptures. This underlying commitment, in turn, is bound to reveal itself in a method in which preachers tie themselves to the Scriptures and, as heralds of Christ, seek to proclaim only that which the Scriptures proclaim.[2]

Thus integrity of scholarship with the Word and personal integrity before the Word combine to produce both a man and a method which can stand before God with assurance.

The Prophetic Element

The second element of preaching identified earlier was the prophetic. In terms of method, the prophetic part of our preaching responsibility is to preach the Word of God with *relevance to the present-day situation* of our hearers.

Everyone needs guidance for living. Practically everyone admits as much explicitly. Those who deny it explicitly (i.e., "Nobody tells me what to do!") nevertheless show their desire for guidance for living through their participation in self-help groups and regular therapy sessions with Phil and Oprah. The closest thing our culture has to genuinely prophetic voices today are occasional colum-

---

[2]Sidney Greidanus, *The Modern Preacher and the Ancient Text* (Grand Rapids: William B. Eerdmans Publishing Company, 1988), p. 15.

nists such as Chuck Colson and George Will or an outspoken TV personality like Ted Koppel.

Some preachers attempt to be prophetic and wind up coming off poorly. For one thing, their hermeneutical-homiletical method condemns them to identifying their own issues for challenge or protest rather than allowing them to rise out of the text. Thus they wind up grinding personal axes rather than interposing a word from God. For another, if the culture presents an immediate issue which begs to be addressed, their method exhibits what I earlier called a bottom-up rather than top-down approach in their preaching.

Knowing that this vague language needs clarification, I have deliberately waited until this point to attempt it. Here is the best case study of the difference in preaching which works from the top down and that which moves from the bottom up. Earlier in these studies, I characterized bottom-up preaching as that which begins with an analysis of human need, explores possible options, shows the inadequacy of those options, and offers Christianity as the solution. As a form of argumentation, this approach to prophetic preaching is hopelessly flawed. Only if one's options are known to be exhaustive and mutually exclusive does this procedure go anywhere. And Christianity can never be the only remaining option to any procedure of ethical inquiry. One could as well argue that since neither an aging Paul von Hindenburg nor a chaotic Reichstag could lead Germany successfully in 1933, Adolf Hitler's appointment as chancellor was the right choice. Was there no fourth option?

Furthermore, the bottom-up approach to such issues as social justice and personal morality is everyone else's approach. There is nothing distinctly Christian about it. For whatever value it has had in any argument historically, it is not unique to faith. And it bears no resemblance at all to the method of preaching used by those people who are called prophets in the Scripture.

Prophetic insight in the Word of God always comes from the top down, and our own preaching which is genuinely prophetic will follow the same pattern. Preaching from the top down begins with a vision of God, explains his character and his relationship to a set of circumstances, and calls for God's people to react to that set of circumstances on the basis of his holiness.

> The Bible is not an assortment of moral precepts and examples. Most of the Bible is theocentric, that is, *God* is the center of the Bible's concern -- God's dealings with humanity, not simply humanity's dealings with humanity. The Bible's concerns are usually more fundamental, more theological, more overarching, than moralistic preaching makes them out to be.[3]

Is the significance of this difference apparent to you? Thus Hosea's explanation of prostitution and adultery among the women of Israel was not their unsatisfied emotional needs in dysfunctional families but the nation's wholesale abandonment of Yahweh for idols (Hos. 4:1ff). Interestingly, Paul gave the same analysis of sexual immorality among the Roman world of his day (Rom. 1:18ff). Don't miss my point. Yes, there are dysfunctional families in the world. The emotional barrenness of relationships in those families certainly contribute to adolescent sexual activity among the children of those homes and the involvement of adult partners in extramarital affairs. But the prophetic

---

[3]Willimon, *Integrative Preaching*, p. 76.

word about sexual immorality is still a call to encounter with God. A realization of a believer's oneness with God through Christ. An awareness that his or her body is indwelt by the Spirit of God. Isn't that the Pauline word on sexual immorality in 1 Corinthians 6:12ff?

The prophetic word to young people and married couples in our churches about immoral sex is not the fear of discovery, pregnancy, or sexually transmitted disease. It is this: "You are not your own; you were bought at a price. Therefore honor God with your body" (1 Cor. 6:19b-20).

Moving from the top down, it is possible to bring an authoritative word from God to people's lives. What is said to them has the authority of God, is rooted in his concern for us, and challenges people at the level of meaningful discipleship. Quoting Willimon again:

> So the sermon is not merely an exercise in telling people what they ought to do or be. Such preaching invariably perverts God's grace into a human achievement, something attained by being nice little boys and girls rather than something that comes as an unmerited gift of God's love. As Keck says, the end result, 'tends to be either a distressing trivialization of the Bible into reasonable advice for individuals, or a shrill demanding of absolutes for the church and society.'[4]

Preaching which is prophetic always makes some claim on the hearers. It sounds a note of authority. It calls for the engagement of the will. It seems likely that every sermon -- even those which are from texts which are principally pastoral or priestly in nature -- requires an element of

---

[4]Ibid.

the prophetic tone to be heard. This is the part of the sermon which answers the question "So what?" Farmer insists that a sermon

> . . . has not been a sermon, unless it carries to the serious hearer something of a claim upon, or summons to, his will, to his whole being as this gathers itself together in the will. A sermon, as we have already hinted, should have something of the quality of a knock on the door. . . . We preachers might well have inscribed over our desks, the master text of all sermons as it were the words: 'Behold I stand at the door and *knock.*' Yet how many sermons I have heard which lack this summoning note almost entirely. They begin, they trickle on, they stop, like the turning on and turning off of a tap behind which there is no head of water.[5]

Again, the only sure way for preaching to maintain this prophetic character consistently is to preach the Scriptures. Expository preaching and preaching authoritatively become synonymous at this point. Topical sermons with proof texts galore may be delivered with an authoritarian stridency which exhibits bombastic disdain for the hearers; expository sermons weave an authoritative message from the top down and affirm the hearers are people who are capable of hearing a word from God.

The Priestly Element
The third element of preaching already specified is the priestly element. This is the responsibility a preacher

---

[5]H. H. Farmer, *The Servant of the Word* (Philadelphia: Fortress Press, 1942), pp. 44-45.

has to make preaching a part of the church's worshipful experience, to make it relevant to the equipping of God's people for ministry, and to cause the Word of God to come alive for Christians in events of congregational import. The relevant method for such a work is *communal celebration* of the presence of Christ.

First, think about the word "communal" and its implications. The church is the body of Christ which is made up of many interrelated members (1 Cor. 12:12ff). When the Word of God is preached, it should have the effect of drawing the body together in its oneness. Affirming unity. Creating a sense of community.

Community is based on a shared identity, life purpose, and vision for the future. The shared identity grows from the sense that the members of the body of Christ are made so through the salvation we share in him (cf. Jude 3a); all born of the water and the Spirit, all indwelt by the same Spirit, and all partakers in the hope, we are a single fellowship under Christ. The shared life purpose centers on transformation by the Holy Spirit into the likeness of Jesus Christ (cf. 2 Cor. 3:18); each believer understands the desire of every other to be Christ-focused in all aspects of daily living. The shared vision for the future anticipates final victory over death and entrance into the kingdom of God in its fullness (cf. 1 Cor. 15:50-57); the church sees itself as in an intermediate state between the defeat of sin at the cross and the full celebration of that victory in heavenly glory.

The most effective way to create this sense of oneness within the church is not merely by being together in assemblies but by having something happen in those assemblies which affirms and nourishes oneness. Hymns are sung together. Readings are done together. Prayers are said together. The Lord's Supper is eaten as an act of communion with Christ and fellow participants. And a biblical sermon draws the church together under the authority of the Word of God for a renewed encounter with the Lord Jesus.

The sermon does not stand alone. It is part of the total experience of the body's fellowship. Yet in the preaching of these sermons week after week, a preacher functions very much as a priest to God's kingdom of priests. He does not so much lay his hands on them or make symbolic gestures over them as he consciously enters into their hearts with the certain message that God not only loves them but has entered into their lives. He has broken the stranglehold of sin on their lives, freed them from slavery to Satan, and delivered them from wrath to come. He has opened not only a fountain for cleansing through Christ's blood but has also given them eternal life and the daily resources for living this new quality of life in a world under judgment. More than that, he has taken them as his partners in bringing light into darkness, good works into an evil environment.

This sense of community does not come about through argument and proof-texting. This approach to preaching is more likely, in fact, to generate internal disputes and disruptions of oneness. It comes about through engaging people in the narrative of God's saving work which unfolds so beautifully in Scripture. Expository preaching generates a new atmosphere in which the Holy Spirit can use the Word as given and as intended to infuse his power.

Second, think now about the word "celebration" and some of its implications. Whatever else worship is, it should not be boring. Whatever else preaching may be, it must never be boring. Worship is the community's celebration of the presence of Christ, and the sermon is part of that celebration. No dry lectures, please. No droning on about irrelevancies. Let the total experience of worship be joyous, and let preaching be alive with divine energy and expectation.

I think sometimes that people from my background know very little of the concept of worship -- and practically nothing of the art of worship as celebration. Perhaps my opinion is only confessional of a weakness in my own heart and has nothing to do with the situation generally among people most like me. Even if that is so, this is the time and place to urge preachers to be creative. Engaging. Interesting.

The gospel is a beautiful story told with literary artistry in the Scripture. We have no right to reduce it to a pedestrian recitation in the context of a threadbare setting we mistakenly call worship.

> Interesting persons make interesting preachers. A person who is dull, uninvolved in life, with a mind as bland as custard, will not suddenly become exciting upon entering a pulpit. While it is true that many interesting people read quite widely, others have sharpened their curiosity about people and life through a wide range of experiences.[6]

In order to fill a priestly role in the lives of people, those people have to believe that you are aware of what is happening in their lives. They have to believe that you live in the same world they inhabit. They have to sense common awareness, mutual interests, and public sensibilities.

Barth's time-worn dictum about preparing sermons with the Bible in one hand and a newspaper in the other is

---

[6]William F. Jabusch, *The Person in the Pulpit* (Nashville: Abingdon, 1980), p. 68.

worth repeating. Read good literature to challenge your own mode of writing and speaking. Read *Time* or *Newsweek* regularly for summary accounts of world events, scientific breakthroughs, personalities in business or politics, and movie reviews. See the films which the people hearing you are likely to see. Be an involved citizen in the community where you live.

As you work your way through the Bible in study, preparation, and delivery of sermons, you will integrate the sacred text with the events of the present day. People will begin to listen who have slept for years. They will even get a sense that the Bible is not so irrelevant to life as they had imagined.

Forget for a moment that the demand of prophetic preaching cannot be done in a world whose people, events, and concerns are outside your acquaintance. You cannot even engage people in mental dialogue, much less help them out of the spiritual confusion they often feel in their lives, if you are out of touch with what is happening. Your priestly role requires involvement with rather than isolation from your surroundings.

Then, since preachers are generally worship directors or central to the process of the larger worship experience, let the creativity, life, and celebration pervade the entire congregational experience. Let people know that the presence of the Lord brings joy, not gloom. Vary the order of service in order to avoid the dreariness of predictability. Incorporate contemporary music which has theological substance and musical quality to it. Some of the short choruses of praise which are easy to learn will do wonders to enlist people in worship. Don't be afraid of change, if change can improve things.

A priestly concern is to nourish, challenge, and involve others. The disenfranchisement which is typical in so many places -- especially of adolescents, young professionals, and young marrieds -- traces largely to our failure in this dimension of our ministry.

The Pastoral Method

The fourth element of preaching named earlier is a pastoral concern. It is our personal concern for and active life involvement with the people who hear us preach. It is loving them enough to do more than preach to them. It is listening to them when they need to talk to us. Cry with us. Disagree with us. Laugh with (or at) us.

The method most critical to pastoral work is *personal vulnerability* to people. It is the hardest thing to allow in our ministry.

The sermon itself can break down barriers and remove some of the remoteness which tends to creep between pulpit and pew. As a text is being explored, it is all right to let people know the impact that it has had on your own life. Let feelings show. Speak confessionally. The pulpit is not to be turned into a self-absorbed man's narration of his life story in weekly installments. But it must be a place where an authentic human being stands with a word from God. That man's credibility will derive from both his command of the text and his disclosure of personal authenticity before God.

If a text contains deliberate humor, such as the sawdust and plank illustration Jesus used at Matthew 7:3-5, play up that humor. Laugh at Jesus' joke! Let your hearers know that it is all right for them to laugh at it. If you are preaching about the reinstatement of Peter to his role in Jesus' work (John 21:15ff), help them feel the sense of pathos involved. If you preach the story of Jesus' encounter with a sinful woman whom he allowed to wash his feet with her tears only to be judged an "unprofessional clergyman" by his host (Luke 7:36ff), you might make it live for someone by relating an episode where you were torn between an uncomfortable personal situation and the opportunity to reach to someone with compassion. People who can illustrate biblical texts from their own lives make themselves vulnerable to others in a healthy way. They show their struggle to receive and live biblical truth. They reveal that they are just like the people who hear them. They become less threatening to approach with a struggle or fear which has become burdensome.

What about telling of experiences which involve other people? Family members? Members of the congregation? If they are to be told with names or distinguishable identities, these should never be used without permission. If there are events which can be disguised for the telling, it is appropriate to relate them as such. They may begin, "This story reminds me of someone I knew that we will call Harry..." That introduction serves as a disclaimer in terms of shielding identity; it also affirms that the essential facts are real.

If the story is *not* real but fictional, say so. You might introduce it this way: "The story is told of a woman who..."

If the story is of someone else's experience, relate it as such. Don't tell an episode from my life as coming from yours. Don't relate what John Doe told of a childhood experience with his father as your experience.

If you are preaching through a book of the Bible or a section of text, don't feel that you have to pontificate on every difficult point of interpretation. If you explore an option or two with your hearers and cannot decide between them, it is good form to tell them so. They can respect honesty. They don't need you to have a cocksure "position" on every difficult subject. It gives them permission to avoid dogmatism when they see you steering around it.

On a Sunday evening in Nashville, an out-of-town visitor came up to me after our assembly with the intention of telling me something. He was rather aggressive. He stood directly in front of me, looked me right in the eye, and said, "You said something from the pulpit tonight that I've never heard in a Church of Christ." "Oh, no!" I thought. What had I said? My mind flashed back through the night's lesson, and I really tried to pull out anything that might have been controversial or threatening. After a bit of awkward head-scratching and saying that I would be willing to talk with the man about whatever it was that had upset him, he said, "It was nothing that *upset* me. It just *shocked* me. If I heard you correctly, you said, 'I don't know.' And I've never heard that from a pulpit in my life before."

Sermons are not finished with the preaching of them. They establish something of a rapport between the preacher and his regular hearers. They form an image of the man as austere or compassionate, out-of-touch or aware, aloof or approachable. Based largely on that perception, people will decide whether to trust you as a person. Do you feel what they feel? Are you serious about seeking God? Are you just another religious phony?

People will ask to meet with you, and the follow-up to your sermons will begin. Some will be so shy and reserved that you will have to probe to find out what is at stake in their lives and why they felt the need to talk with you. Others will shock you with their candor. You must learn to respond to both types in a way which reflects Christ's own heart.

On those occasions when you know you have been the instrument of God, you soar heavenward in your spirit. A specific sermon got someone's attention, and God moved through it to reach that man's heart. Preaching to a certain person over an extended period of time convinced her that you would care about her confusion and give responsible, prayerful counsel; she came, God enabled you to be helpful, and her life is healing now. Your attempts to bring life and freshness into worship through your preaching kept a young couple from dropping out, and five months later they have said so to you -- and thanked you. Someone who was invited to a service by a friend who could honestly assure him, "He will just preach the Bible," has just been baptized into Christ.

Each of these has been an encounter with Christ. And you have played a role. You have been God's instrument. Your preaching has been the event which made salvation possible to those people. Could God have used someone else for those times and places? Of course. But he chose to allow you to be there for him. Praise him! What a wonderful God we serve!

Conclusion

So preach, my brother. *Preach!*

Preach the Word! Looking first to your own life and only then to your homiletical skills, submit everything to the judgment of the Living Word. Handling the Word of God with integrity, let people hear its words and see its central figure through you. With sympathetic awareness of the lives of those who hear you, integrate the powerful message of redemption into the reality of the world which is so confused and confusing without divine perspective. With creativity,

Epilogue

Anthony Trollope was a popular English novelist during the nineteenth century. His most famous books are the Barsetshire novels, six books about life in the fictitious county of Barsetshire. Their tone is mildly satirical, and a good deal of interest in the series focuses on the cathedral city of Barchester.

In Trollope's *Barchester Towers*, published in 1857, the narrator in his imaginary world says:

> There is, perhaps, no greater hardship at present inflicted on mankind in civilized and free countries than the necessity of listening to sermons. No one but a preaching clergyman has, in these realms, the power of compelling an audience to sit and be tormented. No one but a preaching clergyman can revel in platitudes, truisms, and untruisms and yet receive, as his undisputed privilege, the same respectful demeanour as though words of impassioned eloquence, or persuasive logic, fell from his lips. . . . We desire, nay we are resolute, to enjoy the comfort of public worship, but we desire also that we may do so without an amount of tedium which ordinary human nature cannot endure with patience; that

we may be able to leave the house of God without that anxious longing for escape which is the common consequence of common sermons.

With what complacency will a young parson deduce false conclusions from misunderstood texts, and then threaten us with all the penalties of Hades if we neglect to comply with the injunctions he has given us![1]

As you would have surely discerned by now, I have no defense to make for one of us who takes his call to preach lightly. The Bible is not a boring, irrelevant, and lifeless book. Preaching done by someone who understands the Word of God and who knows the needs of his hearers will not be an inflicted "hardship" which leaves people "longing for escape." It will be an ongoing event of encounter between the Living Christ and souls longing for eternal life.

In the four themes studied to this point, I have tried to set a high standard for myself and my peers. Indeed, since we serve the Lord Jesus Christ, the standard we embrace for our ministries cannot be a shoddy one. We must believe that the gospel is God's power to save and that preaching is his method of making that message known to the world.

Yet, while accepting the nobility of our calling and embracing the high standard it demands, we must also be called back to practical reality. We are mortals. We are flawed. We are sinners.

As surely as the call to preach the gospel is a gift of grace, so is the ability to fulfill that call a gift of grace as well. Lest we despair of our mission, then, let us remember where our sufficiency lies. "But we have this treasure in jars of clay to show that this all-surpassing power is from God and not from us" (2 Cor. 4:7).

---

[1] Anthony Trollope, *Barchester Towers* (New York: New American Library, 1984), pp. 59-60.

Sermons

A World of Walking Corpses

What is it to be human? What is the meaning of our existence in the world? Does life have a goal? Is the grave the end of it all?

Miguel de Unamuno, a Spanish writer and philosopher, asserted in his *The Tragic Sense of Life*: "Since we live only in and by contradictions, since life is tragedy and the tragedy is perpetual struggle, without victory or the hope of victory, life is contradiction."

Albert Camus, the French Resistance fighter whose writing won the Nobel Prize in 1957, claimed: "If the only significant history of human thought were to be written, it would have to be the history of its successive regrets and its impotences." In the essay just quoted, *The Myth of Sisyphus*, he is exploring the "one truly serious philosophical problem, and that is suicide."

Bertrand Russell, the English mathematician and philosopher, wrote in his *Mysticism and Logic*: "That man is the product of causes which had no prevision of the end they were achieving; that his origin, his growth, his hopes and fears, his loves and his beliefs, are but the outcome of accidental collocations of atoms; that no fire, no heroism, no intensity of thought and feeling, can preserve an individual life beyond the grave; that all the labours of the ages, all the devotion, all the inspiration, all the noonday brightness of human genius, are destined to extinction in the vast death of the solar system, and that the whole temple of Man's achievement must inevitably be buried beneath the debris of a universe in ruins -- all these things, if not quite beyond dispute, are yet so nearly certain, that no philosophy which rejects them can hope to stand."

Thus have three celebrated thinkers defined the human experience. And they would be correct, *if there were no God.* Moreover, they are right even from a Christian perspective in describing *life which is severed from God.*

When men and women live apart from God, their very existence is a living death and a dying life. The world of these people is a world of walking corpses. And the preaching of the gospel of Christ to this generation must begin with the awareness of *death* as our presenting complaint as human beings and *life* as our proper goal. Until we smell the stench of our own death, we have little real motivation to seek the one who alone is The Way, The Truth, and *The Life.*

Our biblical text for this study is Ephesians 2:1-3. "As for you, you were dead in your transgressions and sins, in which you used to live when you followed the ways of this world and of the ruler of the kingdom of the air, the spirit who is now at work in those who are disobedient. All of us also lived among them at one time, gratifying the cravings of our sinful nature and following its desires and thoughts. Like the rest, we were by nature objects of wrath."

Living Dead Men

Paul could not minimize sin and would not mollify the plight of one who does not know Christ. Our terms might be "misguided," "out of step," or "sick." Indeed, these descriptions may be correct. But they do not go far enough. Beyond that person's intellectual confusion or psychological state, it remains still to identify his spiritual condition. The apostle says that such a man or woman is *dead*.

A physical organism, whether plant or animal or man, is dead when it has no life force. No power for growth and function. The spiritual life of a person is gone when there is no divine presence. No power for purity and holiness. So Paul writes in Colossians 2:13 of people who "were dead in your sins and in the uncircumcision of your sinful nature."

Perhaps even more to the point is Paul's characterization of this spiritual circumstance in a human experience in writing to his colleague Timothy. "But the widow who lives for pleasure is dead even while she lives" (1 Tim. 5:6). The person, whether male or female, who lives for the titillation of what the Bible calls "the cravings of our sinful nature" (cf. v.3) is spiritually dead even if he lives to be 100 years old.

Death is always some form of separation. The body dies when it is separated from its animating spirit (cf. Jas. 2:26a). Faith dies when it is separated from validating actions (cf. Jas. 2:26b). And souls die when they are separated from their God.

The thing that separates a living soul (i.e., human being) from God is "transgressions and sins." Perhaps the two words are synonyms here, as they appear to be in Romans 5:12-21. If there is a difference, "transgressions" (*paraptoma*) are instances of deliberate violation of known law, kicking at the traces, stepping over the boundaries, and "sins" (*hamartia*) are occasions of missing the mark, stumbling, failing. But would the latter really be evil? How could our mistakes separate us from God?

A few years back the following story appeared on the front page of *USA Today*. A flight headed from Charlotte, North Carolina, to Augusta, Georgia, missed the landing site. The 737 landed six miles from Augusta's primary airport at a little field with short runways which are inadequate for a jumbo jet. With brakes screeching and engines roaring, the plane left skid marks for half the length of a 3,800-foot runway. But here's the most astonishing part of the story. A spokesman for the airline commented on the possibility of disciplining the plane's pilot by saying, "On balance, he did more right things than wrong things." Can you believe it? He landed at the wrong airport, but it was a great landing!

Maybe that defense came to mind instantly for the airline spokesman, for some form of defensiveness seems to be the universal response for human failure. "Yes, I ate the forbidden fruit," said Adam, "but the woman you put here gave it to me." "Yes, I took the money," says the thief, "but I was entitled to it because of all the bad breaks I've gotten in my life." "Yes, I had the affair," says the man, "but you don't know what it has been like to have to live with my demanding, whining wife." And on and on it goes. We all admit to missing the mark but somehow tend to feel that, on balance, we did more that was appropriate to the circumstance than was genuinely immoral. That very defensiveness in our failures is why not only our deliberate transgressions but even our "innocent mistakes" wind up killing us.

The result of our rebellions against and self-justifications before God is an abandonment of spirituality. A progressive giving way to evil. A conscious moving away from the light of God's holiness into the deepening darkness of everything that opposes him. We become walking corpses who "follow the ways of this world and of the ruler of the kingdom of the air." It is the story I have had told to me a thousand times. More than that, it is the experience I have lived.

Though created by God and though it will be ultimately revealed as subject to his sovereignty, this world is currently under Satan's control. So dominant is the devil in our present environment that "the ways of this world" (i.e., life in the grip of evil) are understood by Paul as positively satanic. It is not only our outright rebellion and our defensiveness in our failures that stalk us constantly, but it is the fact that the very culture in which we live is enemy territory. Avoiding sin is hard enough under ideal circumstances because of its locus in our own misdirected desires (Jas. 1:14; cf. v.3a), but it is even harder when living in a world that glories in evil behavior and taunts the person who spurns its ways.

Planet Earth is in the grip of Satan, "the ruler of the kingdom of the air." In the ancient cosmology of rabbinic literature, this planet's immediate atmosphere was inhabited by demons. Between God's high heaven and the domain under man's control lay the sphere of evil spirits. This province has been called "rule and authority, power and dominion" earlier in the same epistle (1:21) and will later be called "the spiritual forces of evil in the heavenly realms" (6:12). Although Christ has defeated Satan and his hosts (cf. 1:20-22), those who are still outside of Christ are still in captivity to the devil. Those who have not yet come into the life of Christ are still spiritual corpses walking about in death. They are "separate from Christ . . . without hope and without God in the world" (2:12).

Perfectly Wretched Creatures

The study of human nature can be disheartening. When you confine that study to *fallen* human nature, as Paul has in Ephesians 2:1-3, it is positively depressing.

The Bible begins the story of humanity on a high note. Males and females of the race are created in God's own image (Gen. 1:27). They are but "a little lower" than the angels and "crowned . . . with glory and honor" (Psa. 8:5). To be human is to be an embodied personality who is self-conscious, morally free, and capable of fellowship with God. It is an exalted standing within the created order.

Yet the story hardly gets off the ground before something goes terribly wrong. The original man and woman use their freedom to rebel against God, and the die is cast for the race henceforth. Adam and Eve died spiritually, as symbolized in their banishment from the Garden of Eden. Their free and open fellowship with God was over. Furthermore, denied an approach to the Tree of Life which was in their original paradise home, they and their descendants have had to face the inevitability of physical death.

The march of the human race has been to the cadence of death since Eden. Spiritually dead people have marched unerringly toward first the grave and then hell. And the paradox of a world of walking corpses has not been lost on these self-conscious creatures. Jesus himself used this enigmatic metaphor when he told a would-be disciple who was concerned to go and bury his father at the heyday of his earthly ministry, "Let the dead bury their own dead, but you go and proclaim the kingdom of God" (Luke 9:59-60).

Paul had a word in his vocabulary which he characteristically used for earth-bound human nature. It was his term of reference for one who is in sin's stranglehold. The word is *sarx*.

For the Apostle to the Gentiles, *sarx* was the word for human nature in its fallen state. *Sarx* is the enemy within. *Sarx* is the death principle at work in us. *Sarx* is unspiritual and the precise opposite of being a Christian. *Sarx* is man cut off from God.

Our English versions struggle to translate *sarx* into our vocabulary and understanding. Both the King James and Revised Standard Versions use the word "flesh." But that tends to make us think in terms of Greek dualism which sees something evil in matter itself. "Flesh" as tissue, sinew, and bone is not evil. So other translations offer "unspiritual nature" or "carnal attitude." The New International Version uses "sinful nature," and only a term that strong is adequate.

From Paul's point of view, the study of *human* nature is the study of the race's *sinful* nature. It is a nature derived from habit and choice, not from inheritance. It is our nature as we have fashioned it and not as God meant it to be. Our sinful nature is human nature as it has become through both deliberate violation of the divine will (*paraptoma*) and missing the mark of divine holiness (*hamartia*).

Read Paul's most detailed characterization of the sinful nature of man and see your own experience in his words: "Those who live according to the sinful nature have their minds set on what that nature desires; but those who live in accordance with the Spirit have their minds set on what the Spirit desires. The mind of sinful man is death, but the mind controlled by the Spirit is life and peace; the sinful mind is hostile to God. It does not submit to God's law, nor can it do so. Those controlled by the sinful nature cannot please God" (Rom. 8:5-8).

In our text from Ephesians, this same picture of fallen human nature is clearly in view. The walking corpses of this passage are not animated by the Holy Spirit of God but by "the spirit who is now at work in those who are disobedient." This "spirit" is anything but holy. It is the satanic spirit of rebellion against God which produces disobedience rather than obedience, thus death instead of life.

People who live by this death-dealing spirit have an ungodly agenda for their lives. Their fatal attraction is for "gratifying the cravings of our sinful nature and following its desires and thoughts" (v.3). Thus the liar and thief, drunkard and gambler, prostitute and homosexual, drug trafficker and corrupt public official. Each is hostile to God, cannot submit to God's law, and cannot please God. All are enslaved to their sinful nature. The power of choice which allowed them to be truly human has been lost to some overpowering craving (*epithumia*). They are powerless now. They are reduced to walking corpses. They are real-life counterparts to the mythical "zombies" of horror literature and superstition; they are dead people still up and walking around.

Tracing this fallen nature to the bitter end, Paul insists that people living out its agenda are "by nature objects of wrath." That is, they are the appropriate objects of divine wrath. They deserve God's judgment. They are due the full wages of sin, which is death (Rom. 6:23). The living death they are experiencing now will become the eternal death of *gehenna*.

The wrath of God is not some subjective response of God to our rebel deeds. Wrath is not what comes from God when he is provoked to the degree that his love is overridden with rage. Divine wrath, unlike the human reaction we call wrath, is holy, loving, and objective. It is not the chilling, unforeseen consequence of pushing God too far but the predictable, necessary corollary to sin within a world created by a God who is holy.

There is an ingrained spiritual symmetry to the universe God has created. Call it a "spiritual ecology," if you will. As with the ecology of our physical world, violations of the balance of our spiritual ecology have disastrous effects. Our sin jerks a great disruption into the spiritual order of things. That disruption, along with the consequences of it for time and eternity, is God's wrath. Objective rather than subjective. Necessary rather than optional. Certain rather than capricious. It is his mandatory and unalterable antagonism toward everything that is opposed to his holy character and righteous will.

To look at ourselves as we have become in contrast to what we were created to be makes us cry aloud with Paul: What wretched creatures we have become! Who will deliver us from this body of death? (Rom. 7:24).

The Insufficiency of Our Sufficiency

Is the scene too gloomy for you? Do you prefer to fall back on the banalities of our time which explain away this sorry plight of ours? Make it unavoidable and necessary? Make it into our opportunity to be all we can be and to rise above our self-imposed limitations?

Balderdash! At the best we will ever be under our own power, we are too bad to approach a holy God. When all our self-help methods are exhausted, that is all we will be for our efforts. *Exhausted.* Not salvaged. Not recovered. Not alive.

But why must the story of redemption begin with such a melancholy reflection on death? Because the first step to salvation is brokenness. Seeing ourselves as we really are. Abandoning the foolish notion that we are all right just as we are or that we can fix whatever may be wrong with us. A little tinkering here. An adjustment there. Then we will have solved our problems by our own efforts. It has been the delusion of the human race through the millennia!

In his famous *Pensees*, Blaise Pascal wrote: "The greatness of man is that he knows himself to be miserable. A tree does not know itself to be miserable. The miseries themselves prove man's greatness. They are the miseries of a great lord, of a deposed king. . . . The man who knows God but does not know his own misery becomes proud. The man who knows his own misery but does not know God ends in despair. . . . The knowledge of Jesus Christ constitutes the middle course, because in him we find both God and our own misery. Jesus Christ is therefore a God whom we approach without pride and before whom we humble ourselves without despair."

It is true universally. There are no exceptions. In our text, Paul spoke in verses one and two of the spiritual deadness of the Gentiles: "As for *you, you* were dead in *your* transgressions and sins, in which *you* used to live when *you* followed the ways of this world . . . ." But he admitted that it was no different for Jews such as himself at verse three: "All of *us* also lived among them at one time, gratifying the cravings of *our* sinful nature . . . ."

Gentile and Jew. Rich and poor. Old and young. Communist and capitalist. Male and female. President and powerless. We are all the same. Fallen. Enslaved. Dead. Damned.

Not one of us can see Christ as Savior until the self-idol falls, so it is necessary that the story of redemption begin with the reality of the human condition. The cross is *good news* only to those who know the *bad news* of our hopelessness without divine intervention.

Conclusion

Can anything be done to rescue us from such a dismal state and from the wrath it dictates? Look back in Ephesians and read of God's "incomparably great power for us who believe" (1:19). Or look ahead from our text and hear Paul celebrate "the incomparable riches of [God's] grace expressed in his kindness to us in Christ Jesus" (2:7).

Against the backdrop of our human insufficiency stands the all-sufficiency of the Lord Jesus Christ.

Against our domination by the sinful nature and its cravings, he stands holy and without sin. Against our inability to honor divine law because of the weakness brought on by our sinful nature, he has honored the righteous requirements of the law fully. Against our sinfulness and guilt and separation from God, he has offered himself as the atoning sacrifice and tasted the horror of eternal separation from God while hanging on a Roman cross.

Against the death of human experience given over to the spirit of evil, he gives life through the Holy Spirit living in his redeemed people. Against the power of Satan to enslave and to damn by tantalizing the cravings of our sinful nature, his Spirit leads men and women to be the children of God.

Separated from its God by sin, this world of walking corpses is utterly and eternally without hope. "But now in

Christ Jesus you who once were far away have been brought near through the blood of Christ" (Eph. 2:13).

On a tablet in the pedestal of the Statue of Liberty are these words from "The New Colossus," a poem by Emma Lazarus:

"Keep ancient lands, your storied pomp!" cries she
    With silent lips. "Give me your tired, your
    poor,
Your huddled masses yearning to breathe free,
    The wretched refuse of your teeming shore.
Send these, the homeless, tempest-tost to me,
    I lift my lamp beside the golden door!"

From these three verses in Ephesians, one might hear these words to the lost masses of humanity as the cross comes into view:

"Keep proud mortals, your vaunted egos!" cries he
    With pierced brow. "Give me your empty, your
    broken hearts,
Your Satan-bound victims yearning to be free,
    The walking corpses of your sinful strife,
Send these, the lost, hell-bound to me,
    My cross has become their thoroughfare to
    life."

How Could He Love Me?

The opening three verses of Ephesians 2 describe the plight of man separated from God. In summary, these verses say that life which is severed from God is no life at all. Men and women estranged from God are fallen creatures whose world has been plunged into wretchedness. And anything that we would offer and boast of as sufficient to change our plight before a holy God is altogether insufficient for any such purpose.

As Paul wrote these lines, it must have brought back painful memories to him of his own past. There had been a time in his life when he fought against God's Christ. When he persecuted and killed Christians. When he was one of the fitting "objects of [God's] wrath." As his original readers read these lines, they must have had their flashbacks, too.

These verses picture the human race dominated by evil forces which are too strong for it to conquer. They portray our weakness and hopelessness before them. Satan, evil desires, alcohol, immoral relationships, addictive behaviors -- these things sap the spiritual life out of us. At the same time, however, these verses contain a glimpse of the power of God to quicken lost sinners and to bring spiritually dead men and women back to life.

God's answer to death is life. His response to the grave is resurrection. His rejoinder to Satan's evil designs against the human race is Christ's redemptive action. In this lesson, we will examine the background of Christ's saving work and try to understand something of the divine motivation which underlies it.

When one begins to get a handle on what God has done to save her or him, a question arises which cannot be stifled. It haunts the mind and reverberates through the soul. *Why would heaven go to such lengths for me?* The answer comes back that God has come among us and gone to the cross on our behalf because of love. Then comes the question of questions: *But how could God love me?*

Paul and the original readers of these words are not the only ones whose minds are sent racing by thinking back to the past. What is in your past? What memories flood your mind which make it hard to believe that God could love you? My own heart starts to tremble at the reading of these lines.

I am a rebel and a scoundrel. I have defied God's authority over my life and have gone my own self-willed way. There is no claim I can make on him. There is no debt he owes me. There is nothing in it for him in loving and saving me. Can it be true that he does, in fact, love this world of walking corpses?

A few years before his death, Karl Barth came to the United States to present a series of lectures. Following one of his presentations, a student asked the sort of question one might expect from Barbara Walters in a television interview. "Dr. Barth," he said, "what is the greatest thought that has ever passed through your mind?"

The still-brilliant theologian paused for a long time to think about his answer. Then, with elegance and power, he said, "Jesus loves me. This I know, for the Bible tells me so." Do you know a more profound thought than this one? Let's explore a text which centers on it.

The text for our study is Ephesians 2:4-5. "But because of his great love for us, God, who is rich in mercy, made us alive with Christ even when we were dead in transgressions -- it is by grace you have been saved."

When God Enters the Picture

One does not have to believe the Bible to know that the human condition is a sorry one. We have polluted our planet and are systematically raping our environment. Greed has caused us to overstep all the bounds of responsibility and civility in human relationships. Selfishness and pride have destroyed countless marriages. Even religion, perhaps *especially* religion, has been turned into a scheme for exploiting the many by the self-aggrandizing few.

Fallen man admits the problem, but he has no means for dealing with it. His agenda for attempting to set his own world right is summed up in the ideology of *secularism.*

The word "secular" is not a dirty word. The adjective simply describes something as belonging to the present world. It points to the field of human work and exploration. We cannot escape secularity, for it is the context of our lives as human beings.

But the term "secularism" embraces much more. It is a closed world view which interprets all things in anti-theistic categories. In "Humanist Manifesto II" (1973), belief in a personal, "prayer-hearing God" is derided as "an unproved and outmoded faith." Signers of the document announced that they could "discover no divine purpose or providence for the human species." Thus they insisted: "No deity will save us; we must save ourselves."

But how? By what process? And to what end? On the view of secularism, death is final. Whatever love or wisdom or creativity or community anyone experiences in this world ends at the grave. It will never be fulfilled. Even the aspiration to do so is a cruel delusion. And the suffering that so many people have to endure in this life is simply a brute, cruel fact. Nothing ultimate issues from it, and there can be no redemption from it. There can only be an end. The End!

The fact that secularism is such a pessimistic and dead-end ideology does not prove its falsity, and I draw out its implications with no such claim. I am simply pointing to the contrast between world views. Secularism may succeed in banishing Christmas pageants from public schools, objective moral judgments from Wall Street, and Judeo-Christian restraint from sexual behavior, but it has no positive agenda for responding to our deepest needs. Christianity, by contrast, sees human life in relation to God and his will. Death is not final, and the eternal fellowship of God to which we are invited outweighs and justifies all that has been experienced along the way.

All this is simply to say that secularism is impotent. It can protest and rail against God, biblical ethics, and the church. Much of what it claims is true, for the abuses it cites in history are also denounced by prophets as well as by atheists. The fault is not God's that we human practitioners of faith are so flawed in our performance and sometimes simply hypocritical in our exploitation of it.

God is *not* impotent in relation to human need. He takes the initiative to do what we cannot do. He acts. He changes things. Against the bleakness of our lostness, he seeks us. Against the misery of our plight, he finds us. Against the spiritual deadness of our lives separated from him by sin, he saves us and makes us alive in Christ.

Secularism sees man adrift on the cosmic sea. Hopeless. Destined only for death and the grave. Mocked by his yearning for something to rescue him. Christianity sees the same man adrift on the same cosmic sea, but it sees hope on the horizon. It sees death as having been conquered. It sees the yearning for salvation satisfied at the cross.

God cares about the human condition. Aristotle's god may be an "unmoved mover" who is untouched by the universe which centers on him. The God of the prophets and apostles is distressed by the plight of creatures made in his own image. He is not passive, and he is not untouched by the pains of men and women.

In the Old Testament, he is certainly pictured as a concerned and feeling God. He is represented as experiencing human emotions of compassion, pity, and yearning. Heschel is surely correct to say that these frequent anthropopathisms (i.e. ascribing human emotions to God) help us comprehend that "the most exalted idea applied to God is not infinite wisdom, infinite power, but infinite concern."

Thus Yahweh was "grieved" in Noah's day that he had made man, and "his heart was filled with pain" (Gen. 6:6). Later, when Israel served idols in the days of the judges, God was "angry with them" and let them reap the wrath due their sin (Judg. 10:7). Then, when they put away those gods and pleaded with Yahweh to rescue them, "he could bear Israel's misery no longer" and acted through Jephthah to deliver them (Judg. 10:16). And in one of the most moving passages in the Old Testament, he laments:

"How can I give you up, Ephraim? How can I hand you over, Israel? ... My heart is changed within me; all my compassion is aroused" (Hos. 11:8).

Moving to the New Testament, we see the fullness of God's glory revealed in Jesus. And part of that revelation has to do with his real concern for those in the flesh with whom he had come to identify. Seeing people who were "harassed and helpless, like sheep without a shepherd," Jesus "had compassion on them" (Matt. 9:36). Beside the tomb of Lazarus, he was "deeply moved in spirit and troubled" and "wept" (John 11:33, 35). Jesus "suffered when he was tempted" (Heb. 2:18), and we can rest assured that he is able "to sympathize with our weaknesses" (Heb. 4:16).

Only because there is a God of power and wisdom could the human situation be addressed, corrected, and set right. Only because that powerful and wise God has entered into our weakness and pain has sin been challenged and its stranglehold on the race broken.

Elie Wiesel, in his book *Night*, has told of his boyhood experiences in the Nazi camps at Auschwitz, Buna, and Buchenwald. Arriving at Auschwitz in the spring of 1944, when he was fourteen years old, he was separated from his mother and sister. He never saw them again.

Wiesel tells of a young boy, "a child with a refined and beautiful face . . . a sad-eyed angel," who was first tortured and then hanged by camp guards. Just before the boy was hung, he heard someone behind him ask in a whisper, "Where is God? Where is he?" Hundreds and hundreds of prisoners were forced to watch the hanging-murder. Then they were forced to march by and look him in the face. Wiesel writes that he heard the same voice ask again, "Where is God now?" Then, he continues, "And I heard a voice within me answer him: 'Where is he? Here he is -- he is hanging here on this gallows . . . .' "

Just as Caiaphas prophesied without realizing it when he told the Sanhedrin that it would be "better . . . that one man die for the people than that the whole nation perish" (John 11:50), Wiesel has come very near the same thing here. His anger and pain over his experiences left him, to use his own words, "terribly alone in a world without God and without man." He is not a Christian. But what if he could see God on the gallows in Jesus Christ? What if he could view the cross as God's entry into our pain? His vicarious suffering for our sins? His solution to our lostness?

That is how I see it as a believer. It is how I must communicate Jesus to you. I want you to believe that God knows the awfulness of human lostness, that he feels our pain, that he came among us to take our sin to himself, and that his death is the means to your life.

What we cannot do, God has done. The problems secularism can see but cannot solve, God has taken to himself and answered in the cross. Things might have gone forever and for all people from bad to worse to hell. But God entered the picture, and things have changed.

Three Little Words

Now that the cross has been brought into view as God's response to our need, we are still left with the question of motivation. Why would God permit himself to feel our pain? Why subject himself to frailty, suffering, and death? Why tolerate the cross?

Our text from Ephesians 2 supplies the motive for God's actions with three words: love, mercy, and grace.

First, "because of his great *love* for us . . ." (v. 4a).

Love (Gk, *agape*) is caring and concern, a willingness to sacrifice of oneself for another. Augustine once called the cross a "pulpit" from which Christ preached God's love to the world. Oh, it is that all right. It is the most incredible pulpit ever chosen. The broken, bleeding Son of God died on a Roman cross as an eternal proclamation of love.

Jason Tuskes was a 17-year-old honor student in high school. He was very close to his mother, wheelchair-bound father, and younger brother. He was an expert swimmer and loved to scuba dive. His final dive was in west-central Florida, not far from his home. He left home on a Tuesday morning to explore a spring and underwater cave. His plan was to be home in time to celebrate his mother's birthday by going out to dinner with his family that night.

Jason got lost in the cave he was exploring. Then, in his panic, he apparently got wedged in a narrow passageway. He ran out of air and drowned. When he realized he was trapped and doomed, he shed his yellow metal air tank and unsheathed his diver's knife. With the tank as tablet and the knife as pen, he wrote one last message to his family. Etched on the tank were these words: "I love you Mom, Dad and Christian."

Over the centuries, "God spoke to our forefathers through the prophets at many times and in various ways" (Heb. 1:1). They seldom listened. Even when they did hear God, they often defied him. "In these last days he has spoken to us by his Son" (Heb. 1:2). And how do we treat the Son of God? We seldom listen. When we do, we frequently choose to defy him. So the Sermon on the Mount goes unheeded. The messages from his parables fly past us. The things we hear in spite of ourselves more often simply aggravate us rather than change us.

But his final message, his dying communication, the meaning of his last few hours, minutes, and seconds -- surely we can't be detached and indifferent to that. Surely we will pay attention to the last communication from the final messenger of heaven to the human race before Judgment.

God's final words to us are etched on a Roman cross. They are blood red. They scream to be heard. They are not the formal words of a last will and testament. They are not the outraged ones of an innocent victim. They are not the anathemas of an angry judge. They are the generous, affectionate, merciful words of divine self-disclosure and hope.

Do you hear the words? From the cross, these are the words of God which ring through the corridors of eternity: "I love you. Sinful as you are, I love you. Though you are the one who put me on this cross, I love you. I love you!"

The love proclaimed by the cross is the eternal, self-giving love of God. "But God demonstrates his own love for us in this: While we were still sinners, Christ died for us" (Rom. 5:8). "This is love: not that we loved God, but that he loved us and sent his Son as an atoning sacrifice for our sins" (1 John 4:10). "To him who loves us and has freed us from our sins by his blood, and has made us to be a kingdom and priests to serve his God and Father -- to him be glory and power for ever and ever!" (Rev. 1:5b-6).

Second, "God, who is rich in *mercy* . . ." (v. 4b).

Mercy (Gk, *eleos*) is compassion for the helpless which shows itself in activity for their relief. The word and its derivatives is used 78 times in the New Testament, and Paul (26 times) is especially fond of it. "Even though I was once a blasphemer and a persecutor and a violent man, I was shown mercy because I acted in ignorance and unbelief" (1 Tim. 1:13). "He saved us, not because of righteous things we had done, but because of his mercy" (Tit. 3:5a).

Didn't God know that most people would continue to go their own self-willed way before Christ went to the cross? Didn't he know that his offer to save people through the Son would be spurned by more than would accept it? So why would he show such mercy, if he knew we were going to spurn him?

An old parable tells of a holy man who was absorbed in his morning meditation under a tree whose roots extended out over the riverbank. As he ended his period of reflection and prayer and was about to leave, he noticed that the river was rising and that a scorpion caught in the roots was about to drown.

The man crawled onto the roots and reached down to free the scorpion. Every time he did so, however, the scorpion struck at him. A passerby saw what was happening and said to him, "Don't you know that's a scorpion? And that it is in the nature of a scorpion to sting?" The holy man replied, "That may well be, but it is in my nature to want to save. And must I change my nature because the scorpion does not change its nature?"

It is in the nature of God to do something for helpless people. So, in spite of the fact that most people either ignore his love or reject his merciful actions or even strike back at him, God continues to extend his mercies. No matter what our reaction or response may be, he continues to offer salvation to the most belligerent rebel.

Third, "it is by *grace* you have been saved" (v. 5b).

Grace (Gk, *charis*) is a term which signifies an undeserved gift. In the New Testament teaching about a sinner's justification, grace is pardon by the divine judge who imputes to a sinner the righteousness of Jesus Christ. With love (i.e., self-giving concern) as the motivation and mercy (i.e., positive action on behalf of the helpless) as the means, grace becomes the realization of our salvation.

So important a theme is grace that one entire lesson in this series of sermons on Ephesians 2:1-10 will explore it in detail. For now, it suffices to point out that human insufficiency is the sphere of grace's activity.

In a world of walking corpses where human sinfulness has made our deficiency apparent, in a world where we are by nature objects of divine wrath, in a world where even our noblest intentions and best deeds are dirty rags, grace alone can help us. Coming to God with our own hands empty, we can only receive a free gift from him. We have nothing to offer which can set things right. We can only trust what God has already done through Christ as sufficient for our redemption.

Made Alive With Christ

Do you understand that people who live apart from God are spiritually dead? Do you understand that God's very nature will not allow him to abandon those people without trying to save them? That his love and mercy reach to them with the intention of bringing them into the sphere of grace? Then you are in position to understand Paul's grand affirmation that God "made us alive with Christ even when we were dead in transgressions" (v. 5a).

Paul used, and sometimes apparently coined, a variety of compound verbs beginning with the Greek preposition *syn-* (i.e., together with) in order to communicate a Christian's identification with Christ. Thus a Christian is one who *dies with* Christ (Rom. 6:8; Phil. 3:10), is *crucified with* Christ

(Gal. 2:20; Rom. 6:6), is *buried with* Christ (Rom. 6:4; Col. 2:12), is *raised with* Christ (Col. 2:12), and *lives with* Christ (Rom. 6:8).

Beginning at Ephesians 2:5, he used a rapid-fire sequence of three verbs with the *syn-* prefix to stress association with Christ. In our text for this lesson, he affirmed that Christians are *made alive with* Christ. Once dead in transgressions and sins (v. 1), redeemed people have been made alive. The same divine power which brought the crucified Christ to life has now brought all those who have been crucified with him to life.

This is not the language of mysticism. It is the practical theology of a Christ-intoxicated man who wanted Christians to understand that what happened through Christ was not only historical at the cross but is eternally real in the experience of those who have gone to that cross by faith to accept salvation. This is at the very heart of Paul's theology of justification and sanctification.

I have something in my pocket that was alive, is now dead, and which will come back to life before your eyes. What you will witness in this acted parable is something of an alternate way of making Paul's point about death and life. Things that are dead can never bring themselves back to life, but some of them can be made alive through their union with someone else who is alive. They can experience his life and take it as their own.

Here it is. It is a leather glove. It once had life as a cow. But the cow died and became someone's steak and my glove. Now I cannot bring this glove back to life as a cow, but can I bring it to life at all? Let's see if it can be done with a command: *Glove, live!* Nothing is happening. Let's try threats: *Glove, come alive, or I will throw you in the fire!* Still nothing. It just lies there. Dead. Motionless. Let's try another approach, though, and you watch *as I place my living hand inside it.* It responds now. It moves. It does productive things. But its life is not the old life of "cowness" but the new life of "handness."

Do you see any points of similarity with Paul's thesis? The old, dead person who is a sinner cannot change his status. Commands won't bring him to life. Not even threats. If that person consents to the presence of the living Christ in his life, however, he will come alive to God. He will respond to God. He will be useful for God's purposes. He will not be brought back to the old life of sinfulness but to a new life of righteousness.

When a person who has heard God's "I love you" from the cross is baptized in Jesus' name, the old man or woman is buried. The person who rises from the water is a new creation (cf. 2 Cor. 5:17). The effective power to work such a quickening and transformation is certainly not water. The real power is the Spirit of the Living Christ. Having repented and having been baptized in Jesus' name, that person has received the remission of sins by divine grace and has been given the gift of the Holy Spirit (Acts 2:38). Now, because he is a Son of God, the Spirit of God's Son has been sent into his heart (Gal. 4:6). The indwelling Spirit of the Son proceeds to animate a regenerated man or woman, just as the indwelling hand animates a glove.

Emptiness gives way to meaning. Despair gives way to hope. Death gives way to life. God's love, mercy, and grace have frustrated and defeated Satan again!

Conclusion

Anatoly Sharansky was kept from his wife for 12 years. He spent nine years in labor camps in the Soviet

Union. His activism in expressing his opposition to the Russian system had resulted in a trumped-up charge of espionage and captivity.

At the age of 38, he was included in an East-West exchange of prisoners and allowed to immigrate to Israel in February of 1986. After two months of freedom, he said: "In the Soviet Union I got accustomed to many years of living in a sea of hatred. Now I have to get accustomed to living in an ocean of love."

Sinners who have lived in the kingdom of darkness, who have been walking corpses for so long, and who have had to swim in the world's sea of hatred need to know of God's ocean of love. They must hear of Christ. Oh, they must open their hearts to God's love, mercy, and grace and experience the new life that is in Christ.

Maybe you've been a Christian long enough and have traveled far enough along the spiritual path which is marked by love, mercy, and grace that you have forgotten how hard it is for some people to believe that forgiveness can really happen. That God can love people who are so bad.

"Jesus loves me. This I know, for the Bible tells me so." Have you ever had a more profound thought? Are you willing to let it move you to see, accept, and be made alive together with him?

Life in the New Age

In the summer of 1969, the Woodstock experience proclaimed the dawning of the Age of Aquarius. Something near 400,000 people descended onto a New York farm to be part of what has been variously dubbed "the culmination of a lot of ideals and sensibilities that were the 1960s for a whole generation of people" or "a herd of grass-puffing mud-bathers." Woodstock was originally billed as "An Aquarian Exposition" and was intended to herald the Age of Aquarius as a new era of universal harmony, brotherhood, and personal liberation.

Since Woodstock, its heirs have fashioned a trendy and highly marketable product called the New Age Movement. Complete with best-selling books, crystals, and mantras, it is a wholesale revival of ancient occultism. With Shirley MacLaine, John Denver, and Linda Evans giving their "testimonies" in highly visible settings, the New Age message is being heard by millions. People from all sorts of backgrounds are chanting and channeling.

If anything was ever misnamed, though, it is the *New Age* Movement. It is old Babylonian superstition wrapped up in the glitz of American materialism. And, as Brooks Alexander of the Berkeley, California-based Spiritual Counterfeits Project has pointed out, the "threefold primal lie" which undergirds the system is as old as the serpent's whisper in Eden: death is not real, man is God, and self-knowledge is power and salvation.

In the spring of A.D. 30, a handful of Jewish men proclaimed the dawning of the Kingdom of God. They had been assembled by an itinerant preacher from Nazareth who claimed to have an unshared Sonship to God. They had come from a variety of backgrounds: fishermen, a tax collector, a political hothead, etc. Through their three years of discipleship to Jesus, they had been convinced that he was the long-awaited Messiah who was ushering in the Kingdom of God.

Since that time, heirs to the apostles' doctrine have garbled and confused their simple theme, merchandised the favor of God by selling items ranging from medieval indulgences to religious theme parks, and divided the people who call themselves Christ-followers into warring factions which render each other impotent.

Drawn still by the compelling figure of Jesus of Nazareth, there are people who seek yet to know the meaning of life in the new age of the Kingdom of God. Feeling betrayed by the personal and doctrinal subversions of his message, they still have a passion for knowing him. Being his disciples. Embracing the distinctive lifestyle of one who belongs to him. And someday living in unending, unimpaired fellowship with him.

An early expression of this vision constitutes our biblical text for this lesson. "And God raised us up with Christ and seated us with him in the heavenly realms in Christ Jesus, in order that in the coming ages he might show the incomparable riches of his grace, expressed in his kindness to us in Christ" (Eph. 2:6-7).

The Heavenly Realms

At this point in Ephesians 2, we have moved the spiritual equivalent of countless light years from its point of beginning. In the opening lines of the chapter, Paul was writing of death, disobedience, and demonic dominance. Now his themes are life, exaltation, fellowship with God, and participation "in the heavenly realms in Christ Jesus."

The dramatic event which metamorphosed people who were formerly objects of wrath into repositories of the riches of God's grace is the cross. With the cross as his pulpit, God proclaimed his love to the human race. No mere verbal articulation of love at the cross. No acted parable of divine concern. But the substitutionary death of Jesus as the perfect Lamb of God to take away the sins of the world.

New Testament theology has a strong sense of *identificational actions* with regard to salvation. Thus what one representative figure does can be attributed to all those he typifies. What that figure achieves can be predicated of all who stand with him. Thus, for example, Paul could present Adam and Jesus as alternate fountainheads to mankind. In Adam's sin, we who are related to him by flesh were all somehow implicated and became heirs to sin and death; in Christ's death, we who are related to him by faith were somehow involved and became recipients of righteousness and life. "Consequently, just as the result of one trespass was condemnation for all men, so also the result of one act of righteousness was justification that brings life for all men" (Rom. 5:18).

This same sense of identity with Christ is affirmed in our text. What he has done, believers in him have done.

Whatever benefits have come to him have come to us. The status he enjoys now is also our status.

In the second lesson of this series, it was pointed out that there is a series of three verbs prefixed by *syn-* (i.e., together with) which describe what heaven has done for every Christian in connection with Christ's personal experience. First, God has "made us alive with Christ" (*synezoopoiesen,* v. 5). Second, he has "raised us up with Christ" (*synegeiren,* v. 6a). Third, he has "seated us with [Christ]" (*synekathisen,* v. 6b).

The sequence of these events in Christ's personal experience is certain enough. In confirmation of all Jesus' claims and as final verification that his death had been accepted as the full atonement for sin, God executed a complex sign for us to witness (cf. Matt. 12:38-40). He made Jesus live again. More than that, he raised him up, delivered him from the tomb, and displayed the resurrected Christ to his disciples under a variety of circumstances. Beyond even the resurrection, he exalted the ascended Christ to the highest place by seating him at his own right hand. Made alive! Raised up! Enthroned at the Father's right hand! Christ's saving work is finished, and his victory over sin and death is attested for time and eternity.

In Pauline theology, Christians are identified with Christ in all these events. Thus our victory over sin and death is also confirmed. His quickening, resurrection, and enthronement were real events of history; the corresponding events in our lives, though spiritual in nature, are nonetheless real. As F. F. Bruce writes: "If the raising of Christ from death to sit at His own right hand is the supreme demonstration of God's power, the raising of the people of Christ from spiritual death to share Christ's place of exaltation is the supreme demonstration of His grace."

In his epistle to the Colossians, written at the same time as Ephesians and also counted among the Prison Epistles, Paul traced the same sequence of events. The Colossians material amounts to an excellent commentary on the text we are examining. Like our text, it is littered with *syn*- words which stress believers' identification with Jesus. Christians have been "buried with him (*syntaphentes*) in baptism and raised with him (*synegerthete*) through your faith in the power of God who raised him from the dead. When you were dead in your sins and in the uncircumcision of your sinful nature, God made you alive with (*synezoopoiesen*) Christ. . . . Since, then, you have been raised with (*synegerthete*) Christ, set your hearts on things above, where Christ is seated at the right hand of God" (Col. 2:12-13; 3:1).

Identified now with Christ, we are called to live "in the heavenly realms in Christ Jesus." The term "in the heavenly realms" (*en tois epouraniois*) is critical to the interpretation of Ephesians. In addition to our present text, it is found four other times in the epistle (cf. 1:3, 20; 3:10; 6:12). There is no word for "realms" (NIV) or "places" (RSV) in the original text, and one could as well translate "in heavenly things" or, perhaps better still, "in spiritual matters."

If, as seems more likely from its four other uses than in this verse, this term is designed to make us think of a *place*, then "in the heavenly realms" reminds us that we are to live on Earth with an acute consciousness that our real citizenship is in heaven (cf. Luke 10:20; Phil. 3:20). If, as this verse most naturally suggests, we take it to refer to a *quality of life*, "in spiritual matters" calls Christians to live a God-oriented existence rather than a life which is dominated by worldly pursuits. Looking again to the parallel passage in Colossians for insight, Christians are encouraged: "Set your minds on things above, not on earthly things" (Col. 3:2).

Whichever interpretation one adopts, the practical application is the same. These verses remind us that our experience with the world was deadly. It sapped away all our spiritual strength. Sin killed us, and we were dead in our transgressions and sins. Now that we have been raised from the dead and given new life, our allegiance must shift. We owe the world nothing; we owe Christ everything. Rescued from the kingdom over which Satan rules, we are to live now as one who is a citizen of the kingdom over which Christ reigns.

The Kingdom Life

To live as a citizen of the Kingdom of God is to do something more than "join the church." It is to experience the day-by-day reality of God's presence. It is to undergo the transformation of your attitudes, affections, and behavior -- your total personality -- so that people see Christ in you. Or, to cross-reference Colossians for one last time, it is to make these words a reality in your existence: "For you died, and your life is now hidden with Christ in God" (Col. 3:3).

Several years ago, Ernest Gordon wrote *Through the Valley of the Kwai*. It relates his personal ordeal of spending more than three years in a Japanese prison camp during World War II. It is a fascinating book which turns out to be something of a commentary on religious experience.

Early in the prison-camp experience, there was something of a revival atmosphere. Many of the prisoners turned to God during the first few weeks of their hardship, and they were confident that he would soon rescue them. There was optimism. There were pious affirmations of faith. Then time passed without deliverance. Enemy soldiers treated the prisoners brutally. Then they turned against one another. They fought, stole from each other, and refused to care for the sick and dying among them. They were living a hellish existence.

Then a wondrous transformation took place in that camp. A few of the prisoners moved past their shallow faith in God as a quick-fix artist and began to live a settled and mature faith. They stopped their bickering and began to practice self-giving love. Some of them nursed Gordon back to health from a serious illness. One inmate starved to death while sharing his meager rations to keep another man alive. One went to an undeserved execution in order to avoid having his entire work crew put to death. Some even found ways to show kindness to their brutish captors.

In his book, Gordon says: "Selfishness, hatred, jealousy, greed were all anti-life. Love, self-sacrifice, mercy, and creative faith ... were the essence of life, turning mere existence into living in its truest sense. These were the gifts of God to men." There you have it! Life "in the heavenly realms" displayed in microcosm. A group of men surrounded by enemies and often mistreated by them learned to live a radically different life. Living past their initial motive of turning to God for quick pain relief, they moved deeply into the heart of God. They found strength to endure what would not disappear promptly. They discovered what many believers never have: Jesus Christ is not the brand name of a spiritual aspirin for wounded psyches but the frontline commander of the forces sent to do battle with evil. The weapons in this conflict are not the weapons of physical warfare. They are spiritual in nature and are capable of casting down every stronghold of error and evil in order to "take captive every thought to make it obedient to Christ" (cf. 2 Cor. 10:3-5).

Do we really take conversion this seriously? Have we reduced what is supposed to be a radical surrender of one's life to a formal statement of faith, a baptismal ceremony, and a place in the church directory? Or do we hear the call of the gospel as a call to die?

Maybe it struck me with particular force because it came from such an unexpected source. The book I was reading was written by someone whose denominational teaching and practice are not evangelistic in nature and whose doctrine of baptism is very different from my own understanding of what the Bible teaches on the subject. But several things he had to say about baptism and its relation to new life in Christ were especially powerful and altogether biblical.

For one thing, he called for great seriousness with regard to baptism. Protesting what he called "promiscuous baptism," he appealed instead for people to be baptized with a heightened awareness of the life it entails. "It is dishonest, if not downright cruel, to entice people with rosebuds, lace, sentiment, self-help, and end up tacking them on a cross."

He's right! Baptism is not a pretty ceremony so much as it is an event of self-surrender. Just as one's body is given over to another and put in peril under the water, so one's life is being handed over to God and put at whatever risk is necessary for doing the divine will. "We must now live as dead people who have given up hope in ourselves and the old certainties, people who have let go. Our hearts cling to a different world."

In fact, baptism portrays a death and burial scene for at least two reasons. First, it reminds one of and is a confession of faith in the death, burial, and resurrection of

Jesus Christ. Second, it signifies the death of the person who has come to Christ. The old man or woman has died and is being disposed of in a watery grave.

The author I was reading made his point rather dramatically by writing: "All conceptions of the Christian life that see converts as basically nice people who gradually become nicer ... are inimicable *(sic)* to the way Paul sees it. Nothing less than death will do, nothing less than baptism."

Each of us who has already experienced baptism needs to ask himself or herself about life since then. Did the old self really die? Did the cross become a personal reality? Has life since then been an experience of the Kingdom of God? Have people seen a difference in you which can be explained only in terms of Christ's presence in your life?

My unanticipated teacher is right in declaring: "Baptism is a once-and-for-all experience, requiring only a few minutes to initiate, but taking our whole lives to finish." Unexpected or familiar source, it makes no difference. What he wrote is unquestionably true in light of Scripture. Yet it is unquestionably neglected in our current teaching and practice.

Perhaps the reason we have lost this emphasis is that we have lost sight of another key expression in Paul's writings. Around 200 times in his collective epistles and more often in Ephesians that in any other, the apostle reveals his fascination with the notion of being "in Christ." As surely as a weather vane reveals the wind's direction, so does this expression show a constant direction of Paul's thought. Against our modern preoccupation with "getting in touch with your feelings" and taking an "inward journey to joy," Paul was caught up in the desire to follow Christ. To know Christ. To lose himself in Christ.

An Ongoing Process

You may be thinking by now that all this was possible in the "good old days" of long ago. You are probably even thinking how wonderful it was that in the first century, when the memory of Christ was fresh among men, that his teachings could effect such wonderful conversion. After all, what spiritual alchemy was wrought in the case of Paul! Persecutor becomes evangelist. Chief of sinners becomes leading missionary. Enemy of Christ becomes advocate for Christ.

But don't write off these wonderful possibilities as historical phenomena only. Heaven's work of saving men and women through Christ and initiating them into the new life of the Kingdom of God is for every generation until Jesus comes again. What God did to make alive, raise up, and enthrone Paul and his original readers with Christ served to demonstrate his willingness to do the same for all others of all times and places. God's redemptive work in Paul was performed "in order that in the coming ages [God] might show the incomparable riches of his grace, expressed in his kindness to us in Christ Jesus" (v. 7).

Some first-century phenomena are not repeatable today. But the grandest work of God which was initiated in that historical context was not Pentecost tongues but Corinthian converts, not raising Dorcas from her bier but raising prostitutes and drunkards to heavenly realms, not calming the Sea of Galilee but taking away the fear of death and judgment from guilt-laden hearts. And these workings of God *are* repeatable.

Throughout the "coming ages" (i.e., history in its entirety), God will always be about the display of the "incomparable riches of his grace" to sinners. Specifically, the message will continue to go forth about the grace of God which was "expressed in his kindness to us in Christ Jesus."

The accompanying assurance is that what God did for Paul and his original readers was not only for them but stands as a demonstration of what he is ready to do for all others.

Conclusion

The community in which God's power to transform, liberate, and empower people for kingdom living is demonstrated daily is called the church. It is the outpost where people of heavenly citizenship live in the world. It is the fellowship of people who are experiencing God's reign and who are enjoying the blessings of the Kingdom of God. The church and kingdom are separable as concepts, but they are often indistinguishable in fact and are indispensable to each other. There is no kingdom without a church (i.e., people who acknowledge God's reign), but there is no church without God's kingdom (i.e., his rule in men's hearts).

In such a body, there is genuine fellowship. The fellowship of pain which sin has created in the lives of its various members huddles them together. The fellowship of forgiveness which Christ's blood has brought binds them together in a common salvation. The fellowship of daily encouragement and nurturing makes the group one. In a faithful church, Christ has shown his people the meaning of accepting one another, esteeming one another, and loving one another. Because he has received us, we receive each other.

Because the church has provided a unique framework of loving support to recovering sinners, it is irreplaceable in our lives. We attend its assemblies. We finance its ministries. We sacrifice time to be involved in its work. Christ has purchased it with his own blood. His truth guides all its actions. His Spirit animates its work. His living presence and reign over its members is experienced in its fellowship.

Today's "New Age" mania is a poor alternative to the wonderful realities made possible for us in Christ. Don't accept a substitute for the real thing.

The "G" Word

The doctrine of salvation by grace has an element of danger about it, therefore some people seem afraid to teach it.

As I walked into a public restroom a while back, there was a frustrated little boy trying to tear pieces of paper towel out of a dispenser. He had washed his hands and was wet all the way to his elbows. I walked over and showed him the crank handle which had to be turned to unroll the towel. He was polite enough to thank me. Then, as I turned away and tended to my own business, he began winding the handle for himself. In less than a minute, his dad came through the door to see what was taking him so long. The little boy shouted, "Look, Dad. Awesome!" And at his feet were several yards of paper towel.

Just as the little boy got carried away with his discovery and acted irresponsibly, so do occasional instances arise where someone "discovers" grace only to distort it. The danger is that some will pervert it to mean license. Perhaps others fear teaching grace lest people not change their lives to imitate Jesus and do good works for God.

The danger may be particularly serious for those of us whose spiritual backgrounds are marked by rigidity, dogmatism, and legalism. Grace brings such a sense of relief and security that we are tempted to understand it as license. Set free from the false theology of salvation by rule-keeping, some have embraced the equally false view that all norms and standards of righteousness have been abolished. Quashed. Wiped out.

Paul, the great theologian of grace, tried to forewarn first-century Christians of this antinomian (i.e., anti-law) jeopardy. So, after a powerful affirmation of grace in Romans 5, he raised this rhetorical question: "What shall we say, then? Shall we go on sinning so that grace may increase?" (Rom. 6:1). In view of his teaching that God's response to human evil had been to unleash a torrent of redeeming grace through Christ, he figured that someone just might suggest that still more sin would elicit even greater grace. He was horrified at the prospect. Thus he answered his own question: "By no means! We died to sin; how can we live in it any longer?" (Rom. 6:2).

The solution to this problem is not to avoid teaching grace but to teach it correctly and constantly. Grace is the very heart of the gospel message. So much so that Paul called it "the gospel of God's grace" (Acts 20:24). To neglect this central theme in our proclamation of Jesus would be doctrinally heretical; we cannot be faithful to God and fail to teach that salvation is by grace. To neglect it would also be unfair to those who happen to hear us; people need the assurance of grace in their most trying times.

My father died of cancer six years ago. He lived three and one-half weeks after the malignancy was found and was not even able to leave the hospital to die at home. Within the last week of his life, he opened a one-on-one conversation with me and said, "I'm getting so weak so fast that I know there can't be many more days left for me. I just hope that, when I stand before the Lord, I'll have done enough that he can let me into heaven." I was sitting on the edge of a cot beside him, and his words were like a hot poker rammed into my back.

I shot straight up, leaned over him, and said, "Daddy, you're the best man I know. But you are not going to heaven because you've 'done enough.' You are going to heaven because Jesus has done everything you need. You are saved because of his death. You are saved by grace." For the only time in my presence during his illness, my father cried. Tears rolled back onto his pillow, and he said, "I don't know why I said that. I know I can't be good enough to be saved."

"Daddy, I'm not mad at *you*," I told him -- with tears in my own eyes now. "I'm mad at me and preachers like me who have left the impression with people that their salvation depends on them. Who reinforce guilt in people rather than help them believe in God's grace. Who deny people like you the peace they are entitled to have when they face death."

People need to know the marvelous reality of God's grace in their lives. And there is no clearer statement of the doctrine than in the text for this study: "For it is by grace you have been saved, through faith -- and this not from yourselves, it is the gift of God -- not by works, so that no one can boast" (Eph. 2:8-9).

Grace: An Illustration

The New Testament speaks of grace (*charis*) 155 times, with Paul leading the way by using the term fully 100 times. In Romans, his epistle setting forth the grand antithesis between law and grace, the word appears 24 times. Even in the short circular epistle we call Ephesians, he used the word no less than a dozen times. But he never provided a formal definition for it. Let me begin by illustrating what grace means in the New Testament and then proceed to justify my use of it.

For the sake of my illustration, you must allow a crisp dollar bill to represent righteousness before God. Perfection. Wholeness. (Produce and leave on visible display a dollar bill.) Since God's standard of righteousness can be nothing less than perfection, any one of us who stands before him in righteousness will have to satisfy the standard his holy nature requires. But we are broken people. We lack the wholeness and perfection of God. God's demand of perfect righteousness stands, however, and he cannot accept brokenness for wholeness, transgression for obedience, law-breaking for uprightness. What shall we do? What can we use for "spiritual coin of the realm" or "spiritual currency" with God? Let me tell you about two people in order to answer our common question.

First, let me tell you about a man I know. He left his parents' home when he was 18. It was not a happy parting, for their relationship had been terrible over the previous two or three years. He left home a rebel, and he had no contact with his mother or father for the 15 years that followed. In the meanwhile, he first joined the Navy. There he began to experiment with homosexuality. As he later admitted to me, confusion over his sexual orientation had been at the root of much of his maverick behavior, especially the drinking which eventually evolved into drug abuse, back in his high school days. He adopted a "gay lifestyle," and settled on the West coast after leaving the Navy. When I met him, he was back in Middle Tennessee and dying of AIDS.

He was asking me about heaven and salvation. He kept using words like "worthless" and "miserable" to describe himself. What did he have to offer God? What could he produce from his life to count against the demand of perfect righteousness? By his own admission, very little. To use his own words, he denied that his life was worth "two cents" before a holy God. But since no human being is without some vestige of decency and goodness, let's say that he can scrape together 12 or 15 cents on our arbitrary scale of human goodness to offer God. (Make a stack of a dozen or so pennies.)

Second, let me introduce you to a 32-year-old woman. She grew up in a good family and always lived a decent life. In fact, she was sometimes taunted as a Goodie Two Shoes back in high school for not playing with the fire some of her friends dared to try. She went off to college and met a bright, handsome fellow. They got engaged at the end of their junior year and married within a month of graduation. She worked to get him through professional school, and their two-child, two-car, one-puppy home is the envy of her friends. She explained to me, however, that her life was feeling more busy than full lately. Even with her family responsibilities, volunteer work at the hospital, and annual work with the American Cancer Society, she felt that perhaps the church could supply some of what was missing for her. Now that her children were five and two, she thought this might be the time for them to be started in Sunday School and for the family to begin attending worship. A woman like this must have a much greater fund of goodness to offer God than the man I described earlier. (Make a high, rounded stack of pennies much larger than the first. *Then walk away from both stacks of pennies.*)

Isn't this a reasonably fair way to represent the way we human beings think about ourselves? Judge one another? Assess the value of human lives? I would even go further to suggest that most of us are inclined to seek out people of the latter sort over the former to associate with and to invite to our church assemblies. We probably feel they are closer to God or more likely to become Christians.

This sort of thinking probably lies beneath a definition of grace I have heard from several sources. As a preacher I know expressed it: "Grace is when you do everything you can to please him, and then God makes up the difference." His imaginary scale was graduated from one to ten, and he was of the opinion that one had to get his performance to the level of "eight or nine, at least seven or eight" to have any hope of being accepted when he stands before the Lord to be judged.

That definition of grace is nothing short of blasphemy. It reveals an utter failure to understand the gospel. It is a theological obscenity.

God's message to you is not (pointing to stacks of pennies): "Do all you can do and trust me to make up the difference, if you get close enough." To the contrary, the gospel message is (sweeping pennies onto the floor): "Admit that all you can do is worthless for your salvation and trust me to do it all!" Empty your hands! Turn your pockets inside out! Accept a free gift from Calvary!

The old song "Rock of Ages" teaches the gospel when it says:

> Could my tears forever flow,
> Could my zeal no languor know,
> These for sin could not atone;
> Thou must save, and Thou alone:

In my hand no price I bring,
Simply to Thy cross I cling.

And the song I want sung at my funeral, perhaps along with "Amazing Grace," has the line:

My sin -- O the bliss of this glorious thought --
My sin, not in part but the whole,
Is nailed to the cross and I bear it no more:
Praise the Lord, praise the Lord, O my soul!

By Grace

Our text affirms that we are saved by grace. "For it is by grace you have been saved . . . it is the gift of God . . ." (2:8a, 8c).

Jesus never gave a theological lecture on grace, but he made it the theme of his teachings. Do you remember his story about the man who owed several million dollars and could not repay the one who had loaned it to him? When the man's creditor saw his hopeless situation, he "took pity on him, canceled the debt and let him go" (Matt. 18:21-34).

And what is the Parable of the Prodigal Son except a story about grace? A boy had challenged his father's right to require him to live under his authority. He rudely asked for his share of the inheritance. He went to a far country and squandered what he had been given in "wild living." Reduced to poverty and humiliation, he started back to the one place where he thought he might receive mercy. With a speech prepared about his unworthiness to be called a "son" and asking only to be a hired man, the boy was getting closer to his father's home. Then, still at a distance from the house, his father saw him, ran to him, and wouldn't even let him finish his speech. He ordered clothes, sandals, and a ring. And there was a party that night to welcome home "this son of mine who was dead and is alive again" (Luke 15:11-24). Doesn't the language sound familiar? It should, for it is the same language Paul used in our larger text. "But because of his great love for us, God, who is rich in mercy, made us alive with Christ even when we were dead in transgressions -- it is by grace you have been saved" (Eph. 2:4-5).

Jesus not only made grace the theme of his teaching, however, but of his actions as well. Remember the day some religious folk brought a woman "caught in the act of adultery" to Jesus? Do you recall what he did? Instead of being intimidated into condemning her, perhaps even joining in stoning her, he rescued her from a wicked scheme which was designed to trap him. He refused to condemn her. Instead of condemning her, he forgave her (John 8:1-11).

Then, on the day when wicked men lied about him, spit on him, crucified him, and taunted him during his dying agony, do you remember what he did? He did what he had taught his disciples to do. He prayed for his tormentors (cf. Matt. 5:44). "Father, forgive them," he prayed, "for they do not know what they are doing" (Luke 23:34a).

Grace is perhaps best understood when contrasted with its opposite. "Now when a man works, his wages are not credited to him as a gift, but as an obligation" (Rom. 4:4). Anyone who is still "stacking up pennies" (i.e., trusting his own good works) for salvation has abandoned grace for works. She is trying to deserve her salvation. He is attempting to feel confident before God by creating some sort of divine obligation to himself through good works.

Jesus parodied this approach to salvation in one of his parables. He told about a man who reminds me of several I have known. He was a religious fellow whose prayers told more about him than he would have liked for others to know. He prayed, "God, I thank you that I am not like all other men -- robbers, evildoers, adulterers . . . I fast twice a week and give a tenth of all I get." Another man was praying nearby that same day. "He would not even look up to heaven, but beat his breast and said, 'God, have mercy on me, a sinner.'" This parable was directed to "some who were confident of their own righteousness," and its point was to affirm that only those who trust God's mercy rather than their own good works can be saved (Luke 18:9-14).

The secret to accepting salvation by grace is a real awareness of guilt before God. Seeing myself as I really am. Dropping your defensiveness. Our pride gets in the way of salvation by grace, and the person who has a "larger stack of pennies" (i.e., good works, honors, respect from peers) will probably have a harder time being saved than the one who knows he is spiritually bankrupt. This is why harlots, drunks, and thieves have always been better candidates for the Kingdom of God than the people we traditionally try to reach. They know their spiritual poverty. But preachers, PTA presidents, successful businessmen, and the like find that grace demands too much. It demands that we swallow our pride.

Through Faith

This text also affirms that we are saved "through faith" (2:8b).

This means that faith serves as the conduit, pathway, or channel for grace. Grace is the divine initiative. Faith is the human response of empty-handed consent to God's way of saving us. It is the answer of a walking corpse to the Son of God's "Come forth!"

Please note, however, that this text says that we are saved *"through* faith" and not *"because of* faith." There is one and only one "because of" to the scheme of redemption, and that causative factor does not lie with us. You are not saved *because* you believe that Jesus is the Son of God. She is not saved *because* she has turned away from an immoral life. I am not saved *because* I have been baptized. Nobody is saved *because of* his prayers, church attendance, prison ministry, or evangelism.

The only "because of" in the plan of salvation is Christ's substitutionary death on Calvary. He paid the full price for our redemption in that once-for-all-time sacrifice of himself for us. Whatever *conditions* there may be to our participation in the grace which radiates from that cross are not prerequisites to meet in order to be worthy of receiving it, for nothing with such contingencies could be grace once received. Belief and baptism are, instead, elements of what it means to accept salvation as a free gift -- seeing ourselves as we really are, giving up our efforts at saving ourselves, and a willingness to give up the attitudes and activities that need forgiving.

Faith is not subjective warm feelings for Christ. Using the word to refer to nothing more than a soft spot in one's heart for Jesus, it would be possible to say, "I believe in Jesus, Mohammed, Buddha, and Confucius." Neither is faith the same as self-confidence. Norman Vincent Peale and Robert Schuller to the contrary notwithstanding, biblical faith is other-directed rather than self-directed.

Faith in Jesus Christ is made up of three elements: knowledge, personal trust, and commitment. You cannot trust someone you do not know, yet trust which is affirmed in words is not demonstrated to be real until it produces a life-changing commitment. Think, for example, of marriage. We would consider someone foolish who married a person about whom he and his family knew absolutely nothing; yet we look with equal disdain on the person who drags out a courtship forever because of an inability to make a commitment.

In the same way, faith in Jesus begins with knowledge about him. A spiritual conception occurs when the Word of God is implanted in one's heart (cf. Jas. 1:21). The feeding and nurturing of that intellective faith over time gives rise to personal trust in Jesus (cf. 1 Cor. 3:5-6). Finally there is a spiritual rebirth of water and the Spirit which makes one a partaker in the Kingdom of God (cf. John 3:5). Interrupting the process between implantation and birth aborts a life which could have been and destroys the channel by which grace would have saved a sinner.

Not by Works

Negatively, our text declares that salvation is "not from yourselves . . . not by works, so that no one can boast" (2:8c, 9).

This must be the hardest truth found in the Bible. The most difficult to believe. The one most antithetical to our sinful nature. Our human pride insists on interpreting salvation as some sort of intellectual jigsaw puzzle to be figured out. We would much prefer that it be an endurance contest than a matter of dependence on Christ. We would even rather it be a stockpiling of good works to counterbalance our sins at a ratio of one to ten. We insist on turning grace's free gift into works' just reward. It is an outrageous alchemy of pride that turns the gold of grace into the lead of merit.

God's standard can be nothing less than perfection, yet no amount of our good works can equal perfection. So why keep stacking pennies? Why keep trusting good works to contribute one whit to our justification? The message of the Word of God is that we must come to God with empty hands and pockets turned inside out. There is no spiritual currency we can offer him. We can only declare spiritual bankruptcy and throw ourselves on his mercy by confessing Christ as our hope, dying and being buried with him, rising to walk in newness by the power of his Spirit in us.

Then, after being saved, we cannot fall back on good works without falling away from Christ. Paul once wrote to some people he had converted to Christ and expressed his concern for their security in the faith. They had not renounced Christ. They had not gone back to a pagan lifestyle. To the contrary, they had become religious zealots who were sticklers for uprightness. They had adopted a code of virtue which can only be admired. They had committed to rituals of diet and other observances that Paul had, on other occasions, both recommended to others and practiced himself. What, then, was wrong with those people? They were trusting their zeal, scruples, and ceremonies to save them. "You who are trying to be justified by law have been alienated from Christ; you have fallen away from grace" (Gal. 5:4).

It happens repeatedly over the course of time. The best of people with the purest of motives undermine the gospel. They preach "another gospel" from the one taught by Paul. They teach a rigid pattern of faith and practice which judges harshly, boasts of its theological orthodoxy, and abounds in scrupulous severity. They finally come to trust their interpretations and the system it generates for their salvation.

Putting Fears to Rest

At the very beginning of this study, I referred to the fear some have about teaching the biblical doctrine of grace.

They suspect anyone who uses the word to be advocating the *abuses* some have made of it.

Grace is *not* moral license, for Jesus told the woman caught in adultery, "Go now and leave your life of sin" (John 8:11). Pardon by grace is not an endorsement of what has been forgiven; it is a setting free from its bondage for the sake of a new beginning.

Grace is *not* an excuse for spiritual laziness. To the contrary, it is motivation for doing what rules and guilt cannot sustain. Paul accounted for the productivity of his ministry in the kingdom this way: "But by the grace of God I am what I am, and his grace to me was not without effect. No, I worked harder than all of them -- yet not I, but the grace of God that was with me" (1 Cor. 15:10). It is grace which liberates a flawed person to offer imperfect service to a holy God in the assurance that it is accepted through Christ.

Grace is *not* a justification for refusing to change one's lifestyle. When the prodigal son came home, do you think there was any perceptible change in him? In his attitude toward his father? In his appreciation for the home he had once resented and left? It is grace which permits one to change; it is guilt which drives him back again and again to repeat the same offense.

There is no reason, then, to fear grace. We should teach it. Practice it among ourselves. Call attention to its redemptive effects as they are witnessed in our midst.

Conclusion

Over against all our pride, orthodoxy, and attainments, God says, "Look at Calvary! That is your only hope! My Son and his blood! If you will abandon yourself for him,

I will credit his death to your account. But if you trust anything you do for salvation, you will be lost."

Someone with a big stack of pennies may find it hard to hear what God is saying. Convicts and prostitutes may enter heaven in greater numbers than preachers and Sunday School teachers, for the latter are sorely tempted to trust what they have done to be worth something to their salvation. That is why an uninvited, sinful woman was saved at Simon's house one day, and Jesus' host remained lost (cf. Luke 7:36-50).

Only those who can admit that all they do for salvation is worthless and Christ must do it all can be saved. Only those who confess that hell is their due can enter heaven.

> Just as I am! without one plea,
> But that Thy blood was shed for me,
> And that Thou bidd'st me come to Thee,
> O Lamb of God, I come! I come!
>
> Just as I am! poor, wretched, blind --
> Sight, riches, healing of the mind,
> Yea, all I need, in Thee to find, --
> O Lamb of God, I come! I come!

Heaven's Crowning Achievement

G. K. Chesterton (1874-1936) is one of my favorite writers. He had a creative brilliance which could cut right through pomp and pretense to bring things into focus with enchanting clarity. He has been dubbed "The Prince of Paradox" and had an incisive wit. Once, for example, a London newspaper asked its readership to respond to the question "What is wrong with the world?" Erudite letters and essays poured in and were printed. One simply said: "Dear Sirs, I am. Sincerely / G. K. Chesterton."

Another anecdote from this man is equally fascinating to me. Sir Oliver Lodge set about to produce a new catechism. Question one was, "What are you?" Question two was, "What then does the fall of man mean?" When they were put to Chesterton, he replied in his typically brilliant way. The question "What are you?" he answered as follows: "God knows!" And to "What then does the fall of man mean?" he replied: "It means that whatever I am, I am not myself!"

What a well-spoken and splendid rejoinder. Would that all of us could live with this awareness of our *identity-as-*

is and *identity-as-meant-to-be* before us. In your more sober and reflective moments, don't you see this same truth?

The precursor of the modern creature dubbed a "Yuppie," the Rich Young Ruler, realized one day that what he was meant to be was greater than anything he had found in assembling a fortune and making his mark in the world. So he went to a Nazarene carpenter turned itinerant preacher and pleaded, "Good teacher, what must I do to inherit eternal life?" (Luke 12:18).

Have you ever felt as he did that day? You know you've missed something. You feel stirrings in your soul which are not satisfied with anything your eyes can see or your hands can hold. Intimations of your immortality quarrel with the trivialities of your daily routine. I think that is what Chesterton meant. "Whatever I am, I am not myself" translates into "I am not yet what I was created to be."

It is this truth which stands at the crescendo of the marvelous ten verses we have been examining from the second chapter of Ephesians. Having begun with the fact of our alienation and deadness on account of sin, Paul has moved from man-as-is through the story of salvation by grace through faith. Now the story which began so dismally comes to a glorious climax with this description of man-as-meant-to-be: "For we are God's workmanship, created in Christ Jesus to do good works, which God prepared in advance for us to do" (Eph. 2:10).

The Necessity of Good Works

Life takes on new meaning, new purpose, *and new behavior* for the man or woman who has been saved. The old person who was "dead in transgressions and sins" is gone.

Buried. Out of sight. In the place vacated by his disappearance stands a new person. It isn't the same old person with a church affiliation; it is a new person who has been recreated in the likeness of Jesus Christ.

Do you need some Bible verses? "Therefore, if anyone is in Christ, he is a new creation; the old has gone, the new has come" (2 Cor. 5:17). "I have been crucified with Christ and I no longer live, but Christ lives in me. The life I live in the body, I live by faith in the Son of God, who loved me and gave himself for me" (Gal. 2:20). "Count yourselves dead to sin but alive to God in Christ Jesus. . . . Do not offer the parts of your body to sin, as instruments of wickedness, but rather offer yourselves to God, as those who have been brought from death to life; and offer the parts of your body to him as instruments of righteousness" (Rom. 6:11, 13).

Do you need theological argument? Consider the New Testament concept of *regeneration*. Salvation is presented in Scripture as remission of sins, justification, reconciliation, adoption, etc. But it is also represented as an act of regeneration (KJV) or rebirth (NIV). "He saved us through the washing of rebirth and renewal by the Holy Spirit, whom he poured out on us generously through Jesus Christ our Savior" (Tit. 3:5b-6). This is the same thing Jesus spoke about to Nicodemus when he told him, "You must be born again" (John 3:7). Reborn and given new life from above, the Holy Spirit is sent into your heart to live and to bear spiritual fruit (Gal. 4:6; 5:22-23).

If there is no newness of life, there has been a spiritual miscarriage between the time of conception by the implanted word and full-term birth. If there is no evidence of Christ living in her, either she has not yet been converted or she has fallen away from grace. If his body has never been taken away from Satan as his instrument and put into God's hands as an instrument of righteousness, he is still dead in sin. If the fruit of the Spirit is not being produced in that person's life, either he has not yet been quickened to life by the Holy Spirit or he is quenching the Spirit.

There is no mistaking Paul's theology of salvation. Just as there is no newness of life apart from justification through Christ's blood, neither is there ever a case of justification by grace through faith in Christ apart from the evidence of good works. People who have been brought from death to life by the power of God are "created in Christ Jesus to do good works." Saved people, to use the language of C. Leslie Mitton, have a "willingness to be commanded, directed, and shaped by God, as well as healed and restored by him, the willingness to obey what we know to be God's will for us as we have seen it in Christ."

Teaching which affirms justification (i.e., right *standing* with God) without insisting on sanctification (i.e., right *living* before God) is false teaching. Jesus mocked that view by asking, "Why do you call me, 'Lord, Lord,' and do not do what I say?" (Luke 6:46). The idea of pardon without transformation is an offense to the cross. "If anyone would come after me," said Jesus, "he must deny himself and take up his cross daily and follow me" (Luke 9:23). Accepting Jesus as Savior is meaningless without also accepting him as Lord.

This must be a "hard saying" of the Christian faith, for fewer and fewer seem willing to accept it. We want all the benefits of salvation without any of the responsibilities. We want the knowledge that we will go to heaven when we die without having to be committed disciples while still living here.

Religion as many practice it is a far cry from what one would expect to see from reading the New Testament. Its focus has shifted from worship to entertainment, from delight in God to captivation with self, from Scripture to possibility thinking, and from spiritual instruction to group dynamics. It makes no demands and has no "oughts" or "musts" in its vocabulary. It praises moral behavior, but it provides no behavioral absolutes and makes morality a matter of passionate decision-making which reflects "authentic personhood."

The result of all this refashioning of the biblical message is the Church of the Warm Fuzzies. It is transdenominational in scope, and all denominations have their occasional society of Fuzzites (or is it Fuzzie-ites?). Warm Fuzzy churches don't hear much preaching of the biblical text and instead prefer threadbare cliches and stories of personal attainment, especially the ones which end on a high note of financial prosperity. Fuzzite preachers read and cite more self-help psychologists than either prophets, apostles, or theologians. Fuzzy worship is more a pep rally than an experience of God's majestic presence.

Fuzziness does not present Jesus as God in the flesh who died for our sins; it offers him as the pinnacle of creative living whose attainments we can duplicate. Neither does it speak of salvation as remission of our sins by Christ's blood; its notion of salvation is freedom from hang-ups and negative thinking. And it requires nothing by way of self-denial, discipleship, or holiness. "Just As I Am" is not the title of a song calling sinners to salvation among Fuzzites but their declaration to God of the terms on which they will allow him to have the honor of their half-hearted allegiance.

Conservative religious people are especially vulnerable to Warm Fuzziness right now. Just as radical subjectivism swept philosophy a generation or two ago as a revolt against ponderous systems which were academic and unemotional, so the same spirit is poised to take the day now as church folk rebel against formality, irrelevance, and lifelessness. The current poverty of many pulpits and the deadness of some churches do not justify a reinterpretation of religion, only a rejection of nonbiblical preaching and un-faithfulness in our churches. Sin is not equivalent to low self-esteem, and the answer to the human dilemma is not an inward journey to serenity based on self-acceptance. Sin is real wrongdoing before a holy God, and salvation is not found in the knowledge of self but in knowing the crucified Christ. And knowing Christ entails accepting a new life which is characterized by good works done in his name and to his glory.

Don't Misunderstand!

Nothing about Paul's emphasis on good works in verse 10 should be taken as a negation of his earlier empha-sis in Ephesians on salvation by grace. What he denied earlier was that good works could serve as the source or foundation of our salvation; what he has affirmed here is that good works are expected as the outcome or conse-quence of salvation. We are not saved by good works, but neither can we claim to be among the saved if there is no evidence of God's presence and power in deeds which give him glory.

Jimmy Moore was a dying man. There just wasn't any future for him. Then he got his chance at life again in the form of a heart transplant at Vanderbilt University Medical Center. A year and a half later, I met him when he was back in Nashville to compete in the Music City Triathlon. It is a grueling event which consists of a kilometer-long swim, a 40-kilometer bike ride, and a 10-kilometer run. The man who had had a heart transplant 18 months earlier crossed the finish line with tears in his eyes and with these words across the front of his T-shirt: "I've had a change of heart."

Saved people have had a change of heart. Our cold hearts have been warmed by the love of God. Our hard hearts have become sensitive to God. Our rebellious hearts have been replaced by obedient ones. Our empty hearts have been filled by the Spirit of God. But that is radical surgery which can be performed only by the Great Physician.

Salvation is by grace and is altogether a divine work. All the glory is God's on account of the cross, the empty tomb, and the proclamation of a free gift. Jimmy Moore did not operate on his own heart. He had to be the willing but passive recipient of a transplant. When the process was complete, though, he got out of his bed, became active in the world, and did things he had not been able to do for years. His goal in undergoing heart transplantation was not to lie in his bed, stare at the ceiling, and remain out of touch with life as it is meant to be.

In the same way, the person who has been saved by grace and who gives all the glory for his salvation to God is supposed to get on his feet, become active in the Kingdom of God, and do things which have never been possible before. Which were never of concern to her before. Which were never part of his lifestyle before. The process of salvation is intended to move him from his as-is condition to his as-meant-to-be condition.

Without the evidence of spiritual transformation which is provided by good works in your life, there is no hard-headed proof that you have been saved. Without them, you are still not what God meant for you to be. Do you offer doctrinal orthodoxy as proof that you are redeemed? So did the Pharisees of Jesus' day. Do you offer pious affirmations of your love for God and man? Talk is cheap! Scripture tells you to love not only with your words but also with your actions. Do you offer someone else's hypocrisy, either real or imagined, in doing good to be seen of others as justification for your doing nothing at all? Then you are a greater hypocrite than the person you indict.

Protest and argue as you will, the "fruit test" of the Christian religion is still the most down-to-earth way of testing anyone's claim that he belongs to Christ. If Christ is in you, you begin to see the world as he saw it. You start to think as he thought. And you behave more and more as he behaved. Your rotten temper is decisively, though perhaps with occasional setbacks, brought in check. Your foul mouth is cleaned up, for no more than fountains gush both salt and fresh water do the mouths of saved people curse men and praise God. Your out-of-control sexual impulses are reined in by the power of the indwelling Spirit of God. You visit the sick and feed the hungry. You pay attention to the loneliest and most frightened person in your community. You help the bad-smelling homeless man, teach a woman in prison to read, or give a child a safe haven from abuse. You might even give your life to take the message of Christ to Uganda or to the Soviet Union.

Why? With all the world telling you it's "dog eat dog out there" and to "look out for number one," why would you give up comfort? Why choose a career in terms of its spiritual possibilities for serving others rather than for its salary potential? Christ is in you. You are a child of the Heavenly Father. You are filled with the Spirit. You used to live in darkness, but now you are in the light. Your mind and understanding used to be corrupted, but now you have been made new. You were dead, but now you are alive.

Again, though, don't get confused. These good works are not saving you. They are not the basis of your hope in Christ. They are the outworking of your salvation. These are not the good works of rule-keeping as the means to salvation; Paul and other New Testament writers despise good works of this variety as futile and pointless. These are the good works of love for God and love for neighbor which spring from a regenerated soul. These are the good works of a child of God which let her light shine before others so that "they may see your good deeds and praise your Father in heaven" (Matt. 5:16). They are the things God will look for in our lives when we stand before him in Judgment (cf. Matt. 25:31-46). Are we welcoming strangers and clothing the naked? Meeting the needs of sick people and prisoners? Saved by grace and awaiting the time when we will stand before the Judge of Heaven and Earth, "let us consider how we may spur one another on toward love and good deeds" (Heb. 10:24).

The one and only source of your right standing with God is what Jesus did on the cross for you. It is by grace that you are saved; it is by good works that you praise the one who saved you. Moral actions spring from a new heart, and wholesome character results from gratitude for forgiveness. It is this insight from the Word of God which remedies the misconception of grace as a license to immorality or as an excuse for spiritual laziness. The high standing of being a sinner saved by grace brings with it the greatest of spiritual obligations.

God's Purpose From the Start

God's original intention for us is still going to be realized. Man-as-meant-to-be is still a live option for God because of the work of Christ. Oh, his intention will not be realized in every one of his human creatures. But it will be brought about in the life of love, right behavior, and good works "which God prepared in advance for us to do." Even if the environment in which he must live is less than it could have been because of sin, the self-forgetful life of righteousness and love which a godly believer exhibits is life as it was meant to be lived.

Such a person is described in another of the Prison Epistles this way: "It is God who works in you to will and to act according to his good purpose" (Phil. 2:13). There you have it. God has wanted to have a relationship with the creatures made in his image and likeness that he could work in them to achieve his holy goals. Rebellious sinners preclude God's intention being realized in their experiences; forgiven sinners execute God's intention in their new lives "in Christ." Every time we encounter this "in Christ" phrase, we are reminded all over again that any good thing which is possible for us is so only because of the activity of Jesus Christ on our behalf. All the glory is his, always and forever.

At Ephesians 4:17ff, Paul grounds a series of practical exhortations to holiness and good works on the fact that conversion marks a radical change in one's life. The old man-as-is may have been ignorant, insensitive, and impure (vs. 17-19). But the new man-as-meant-to-be is renewed, reclothed, and righteous. Thus certain things are expected of him (vs. 20-24). A Christian "must put off falsehood and speak truthfully to his neighbor" (v. 23). "He who has been stealing must steal no longer, but must work, doing something useful with his own hands, that he may have something to share with those in need. Do not let any unwholesome talk come out of your mouths, but only what is helpful for building others up according to their needs, that it may benefit those who listen" (vs. 28-29). It doesn't sound like Paul took grace as an excuse for lackadaisical living but as the mandate for spiritual excellence.

And Peter would later add: "You are a chosen people, a royal priesthood, a holy nation, a people belonging to God, that you may declare the praises of him who called you out of darkness into his wonderful light. Once you were not a people, but now you are the people of God; once you had not received mercy, but now you have received mercy" (1 Pet. 2:9-10). His theme is the same as Paul's in Ephesians 2. The call from darkness into light was at God's initiative and thus was by grace; the result of accepting mercy and status from God is an obligation to "declare the praises of him who called you." He continued: "Live such good lives among the pagans that, though they accuse you of doing wrong, they may see your good deeds and glorify God on the day he visits us" (1 Pet. 2:12).

When such a holy purpose is realized in us, we are "God's workmanship." The interesting word translated "workmanship" here is the Greek term *poiema*. It is the root word from which we get our English word "poem." It is something made, something which displays the special genius of its creator. That is the status of the Christian in the scheme of God. He stands as the demonstration of divine love, mercy, grace, and kindness. She is the finished product of redemptive art.

It is easier to see this workmanship in first-generation Christians. The stark contrast of before and after reminds all of us who see these new creatures on display of God's redeeming work. Every church needs first-generation believers to keep this phenomenon before its people. It evokes praise. It inspires confidence. It attracts others to the God who performs such wonders.

An expanding universe displays his infinite power, but it takes rescued sinners doing unselfish good works to display his infinite grace.

Conclusion

Thus the story is brought to its completion. People once dead in trespasses and sins have become God's workmanship. People who once followed the ways of this world and were busy gratifying the cravings of their sinful nature are created in Christ Jesus to do good works. People who were by virtue of their sinful nature objects of wrath have become what God always wanted them to be.

In all ages yet to come, it will be the one and only story of redemption. And it can be *your* story, too. Praise God. What a difference a Savior makes!